Caring for Older People

A Nurse's Guide

Caring for Older People

A Nurse's Guide

MARY CARROLL

RN, C, MA

L. JANE BRUE

RN, M.Ed., MSN

Editor, UK Edition

BRIAN BOOTH

RGN

© Springer Publishing Company, Inc. 1987
© Brian Booth – Macmillan adaptation 1993

First published 1987 by
Springer Publishing Company, Inc.
536 Broadway
New York, NY 10012

This edition published 1993 by
THE MACMILLAN PRESS LTD
Houndmills, Basingstoke, Hampshire RG21 2XS
and London
Companies and representatives
throughout the world

ISBN 0–333–57295–5

A catalogue record for this book is available
from the British Library.

Copy-edited and typeset by Povey–Edmondson
Okehampton and Rochdale, England

Printed in China

CONTENTS

ACKNOWLEDGEMENTS

The authors wish to express their appreciation to those who have given their support to this project. Our husbands, Jim Carroll and John Brue, deserve special mention for their understanding of the work involved. Special recognition must be given to Gari Lesnoff-Caravaglia, PhD, of the Center on Aging, University of Massachusetts. Without her wisdom this text could not have been written.

The authors also wish to thank their colleagues and the many older persons who contributed to our combined clinical experience of over fifty years. We are also grateful to Dalisey Bello-Manabat, MD, and Gregorio Manabat, MD, for their expert assistance with aspects of this book that involve medical practice, and sincerely appreciate the help of Ralph Bellas, PhD, and Louise Bellas, MSN, with the copy-editing.

M. C.
L. J. B.

The care of older people is possibly the most complex, challenging and rewarding area of nursing. This fact has become apparent to many British nurses in the last few years: managers who were once grateful for anyone willing to work in the speciality, now often find that they have more applicants than vacancies. Where once the dedicated few who had freely chosen elderly care stood out a mile, there is now a growing pool of professionals whose work has benefited all areas of care. Consider the nursing development units, the recognised centres of excellence in Britain: how many of them are elderly-care units?

It is an area characterised by the most rapid growth in demand. The number of people aged 85 and over in England and Wales grew at 3.8 per cent per annum throughout the 1980s; and the 146 000 people over the age of 90 in 1981 is estimated to become over 300 000 by the year 2000.[1] By the end of the century, some sources suggest, 11.1 million people in the United Kingdom will be over 70 years of age – one in five of the total population.[2, 3]

As a result of this increased 'elderly' population, there will be an increasing demand for health care; put bluntly, we are seeing people fall ill with age-related conditions who, not that many years ago, simply would not have lived long enough for these to develop. As a result, there is a growing need for nurses skilled in the care of the older person.

As demand for acute hospital beds rises, the pressure on the health service to reduce average lengths of stay in hospital has increased, with the result that the treatment of people in their own homes has expanded immeasurably. The trend towards increased care in the home is reflected in this volume, which has been designed to be of use to nurses in both 'institutional' and domestic settings. Practitioners in rehabilitation, in continuing care and in the community are being challenged to care for people who are more acutely ill, and thus require complex nursing; they need special clinical skills (including communication skills), the ability to use the nursing process effectively, and, most importantly, a love and respect for older people. All of these are essential to the provision of high-quality nursing care.

Gerontological nursing – or 'care of the elderly', as it is now commonly called in Britain, 'geriatrics' having acquired connotations of decrepitude and poor standards of care – is particularly difficult because older people commonly have multiple health problems; there are also more individual differences between older persons than amongst any other age group. Everyone ages at different rate; one of us recently nursed a 97-year-old lady who had fractured the neck of her femur, but due to her iron constitution, eventually walked off the ward and back to her own home, whilst a 67-year-old lady in a nearby bed would require total nursing care for the rest of her life, due to chronic ill-health. It is vital that we understand differences in functions that occur with ageing, if we are to use the nursing process to best effect.

In the past, the focus of traditional medicine (and nursing) has been largely on the treatment of disease; more than one person has suggested that the National Health Service (NHS) be rechristened the national *sickness* service. Now, however, there is an international trend towards 'wellness-orientated' health care, disease prevention, and health promotion. In the United Kingdom, this is perhaps best exemplified by Project 2000, the national nurse-training programme that is firmly rooted in the health of the individual.[4] Gerontological nurses are in an excellent position to assist older people in the attainment of better health, through functional assessment and nursing interventions that are both supportive and educative in nature.

This book is intended to provide the nurse with essential information in a brief, easy-to-use format for treating common health problems of the elderly. Nursing diagnoses (see the Introduction to part II on page 47) are integrated throughout. In addition to discussing the basic categories of health problems, the book addresses general principles of promoting wellness, including psychosocial considerations, nutrition, and the creation of an environment that facilitates improvement of the older person's quality of life.

Briefly, Chapter 1 begins with the first step in the nursing process: the initial interview and health history. A detailed assessment document is provided as a sample interview tool. Chapter 2 provides information about normal age-related changes commonly seen in the older person, and gives some pointers to physical assessment, approached from the perspective of 'top to toe'. An in-depth physical guide is also provided.

In Chapters 3 to 11, various potential health problems and common pathological conditions of older people are discussed; each chapter looks at possible nursing diagnoses and related interventions.

Chapters 12, 13 and 14 take a more holistic viewpoint, looking at psychosocial, environmental and nutritional aspects of ageing. Chapter 15 offers some guidance on drawing up care plans, whilst the final chapter contains several case studies, followed by suggested nursing diagnoses and interventions.

At the end of some chapters are 'discussion points', none of which has right or wrong answers; they are included to highlight some of the less cut-and-dried issues raised in the preceding sections, and may be of use in less formal teaching sessions as starting points for debate.

It is the wish of the authors and the editor of this volume that this book will be useful, in one way or another, to everyone who has the good fortune to be working in this most rewarding of specialities.

To avoid clumsy circumlocutions, the nurse is referred to as 'she' throughout the book, while patients or clients are 'he/she', unless their gender is relevant to the topic under discussion.

PART I

First steps of the nursing process

CHAPTER ONE

The initial interview and health history

The collection of the health history is the first step in assessment. The purposes of this procedure are to establish a rapport, aiding good communication, to determine the person's expectations of what nursing will do for them, and to gather data for the formulation of nursing diagnoses [see the Introductions to Parts II and IV] and of a plan of care. In the case of a planned transfer from one ward to another (for example, from 'acute' to 'rehabilitation'), discharge to a nursing home, or back into the community, the ideal is that the history is collected before transfer or discharge; members of the multidisciplinary team could visit the person beforehand, meeting later to draw up a preliminary plan of care, ready for the moment the person arrives in their area.

In reality, the possibility of this happening is often remote, chiefly due to pressure of work; a good compromise would be a nurse paying a short preliminary visit, but even this might prove difficult at times. This is a great pity – any nurse fortunate enough to have worked in a unit where introductory visits have been possible will vouch for their value, and attest to the fact that they will, as a rule, *save* time.

The majority of initial interviews, then, will take place shortly after the person arrives at his or her destination. If he or she has come from another ward, then it is hoped that some information will at least have been telephoned through beforehand, and there will be a summary of problems and care to date in a transfer/discharge/community liaison letter. If the individual has come from home, or via accident and emergency, the only written information might well be contained in a general practitioner's letter – which could be anything from a carefully written health history to a few scribbled lines that tell the reader little or nothing. There is no better source of information than the patients themselves, but they may be too ill or weak to tell us anything much, or have profound communication problems such as dysphasia or deafness. This is where the spouse, children, neighbours, or any significant other person is invaluable. If it is at all possible to have such a person on hand at the time of interview, the task of information-gathering is greatly simplified. But there is a note of caution that must be sounded here: we must never forget that a person's health is primarily his or her own concern, and that he or she may not want any other person, however close the links of blood or affection, present during such a discussion. That is every person's right, and we must respect it. Another problem, which some readers have probably encountered, comes when a request for a family member to help with providing background information is met by a phalanx of relatives turning up at the same time, arguing amongst themselves about what month in 1932 it was when the person had his appendix removed, and whether there were nine sutures or ten. If a relative or friend is going to help, it is often wise to ensure that only one or two people are nominated in the first instance.

Care must be taken not to overtax a person who is weak or acutely ill. Often, a great deal of information can be obtained from medical records and previous nursing notes. (There is a growing trend amongst community nurses to send copies of care plans into hospital with people, and this is almost always of great use; it is uncertain how many hospital nurses reciprocate when they discharge patients, but it is an area which would benefit from research.) However, any information from other sources should always be confirmed.

The use of medical jargon in the interview is often counter-productive; for example, 'heart failure' is synonymous in some people's minds with 'cardiac arrest'. If the person is allowed to express the perceived problems with his or her health in his own terms, there is much less chance of misunderstandings.

How we address the person is also very important. Unless invited to do otherwise, it should automatically be Mr, Mrs, Miss, or whatever title is appropriate. Use of the first name, or even worse, patronising terms such as 'honeybunch', is very often distressing to the older person, even though they may not protest. Many of the people we meet over the age of fifty had formality of address, and respect for their 'elders and betters' drummed into them from a very early age.

Only pertinent information need be collected during the initial interview. For example, there is really no point in eliciting a detailed history of childhood illnesses if there is no likely relationship to immediate care, since such information can usually be gathered from other sources. The nursing history should focus on the principal health problem (or problems) of the individual – that is, the reason for needing nursing care in the first place. In addition to this, other areas to explore and include are self-care practices, medication past and present, and a basic nutrition history. The interview should also focus on the person's strengths, coupled with their expectations of care. It is much more positive to stress that someone has full use in one side of their body, rather than say that they have no use in the other; right from the start, we are thus laying the emphasis on health and independence, not sickness and dependence. Faced with a bedfast person with little or no movement in their limbs, say, it might be it difficult to discover anything positive to emphasise – but even if only one ability, such as swallowing, is intact, the positive ability should be stressed.

The nurse can also accomplish a general inspection during the initial interview. Areas that are easily evaluated, normally, are the person's ability to get around, with or without assistance, and their competence in the activities of daily living (ADLs),[1] such as eating, drinking, transferring, using the toilet, or dressing. Obvious pain (or lack of it) should be recorded, as well as some sort of assessment of mental awareness. In addition, things to look out for include skin colour, the existing state of personal hygiene, and their relationship to their surroundings and significant other people.

A good medication history notes currently prescribed drugs, their dosage, route and time of administration; but this is only the beginning. It should continue with the person's understanding of: why he and she takes the drugs they do, special precautions, any instructions (such as whether any drug is to be taken on an empty stomach, or with food), and possible side-effects. Untoward reactions and allergies to any form of medication must, of course, be recorded in an easily seen position. The history should also include drugs that have been discontinued, since high plasma concentrations of some compounds can persist due to age-related changes in absorption, distribution, and excretion times. Discontinued regimes can sometimes provide clues to health problems that the person may not have identified, such as hypertension infections, and epilepsy, to name but a few.

A history of over-the-counter (OTC) medications, including topically applied preparations, can be important. Examples of conditions which commonly give rise to self-prescription include muscle/joint pain, headache and gastrointestinal discomfort. (Many older people still believe the myth about constipation being potentially autotoxic,[2] and take aperients in a fashion that can only be described as abuse.) Many OTC preparations can interact with other drugs, and there is a high probability that patients will continue taking them without thinking it worthwhile to bother busy nurses and doctors with queries – after all, these are things that anyone can buy. One of us remembers a gentleman who was prescribed co-proxamol, two tablets every six hours, giving a daily paracetamol dosage of 2.6 grammes. It was only after the jaundice started that it came to light: he was also taking four grammes of paracetamol a day from the stock he had brought in with him. He thought it could do no harm . . .

Many elderly people have great faith in herbal or homoeopathic remedies, which are not obtainable through general practitioner prescription or hospital pharmacies; if they wish to continue taking these, and a pharmacist can confirm that there is no overriding reason why they should not, it will need to be explained that they may have to make their own arrangements about supply.

Basic nutritional information should include the person's ability to feed themselves, chew and swallow; whether there is a prescribed therapeutic diet (such as low sodium, or high protein), or a preferred self-determined one; and usual meal times. Food allergies or intolerances must be recorded (and preferably re-checked – it is not unusual for someone to be thriving on a 'normal' diet in hospital, when a member of their family informs staff some time later that the person will suffer dire consequences, should they ever eat certain foods). Special dietary practices related to religion or ethnicity must be recorded, of course; and vitamins, food supplements or health foods not revealed in the medication history may come up at this point.

The interview's duration is determined by the person's ability to participate for any length of time; so it is essential that the interviewer concentrates on areas of immediate importance, while other sections can be completed at a later date. There is no hard-and-fast rule here, as every interview will be unique; what is of paramount importance to planning one person's care may be peripheral to someone else's. For example, past family medical history can be of some value in anticipating health problems with a familial component, but it is probably safe to assume that with the majority of people, this section can be left for a later date.

The health history is completed by noting past illnesses, surgery, hospitalisations and any other health problems. Responses should be recorded at the time they are given, and it is wise to verbally paraphrase or repeat any responses that seem unclear.

As we mentioned at the beginning, it will be rare indeed for the history and initial nursing assessment to be completed before admission, transfer or discharge to your area; the first meeting between patient/client and interviewer will probably be in the new ward, nursing home or final discharge destination. It is *not* a paper exercise for gathering information that may or may not be of use, but an opportunity for creating a solid base on which trust between people can be built. This is of much more moment when the person is unfamiliar with their new surroundings. If the interview is to be completed by another person, or different members of the multidisciplinary team, then this must be clearly explained to the person and/or any other people who are likely to be involved.

Any health information forwarded from other agencies (be it an institution or an individual) needs to be carefully reviewed, and if necessary, the originator contacted for elucidation of specific points. For some reason, consultation with other professionals (including nurses) is sometimes overlooked as a valuable resource for planning and providing care.

A suggested assessment document for health history assessment is provided on the following pages. This is not intended to be something that must be worked through, whatever the setting; rather, it can be thought of as a menu from which practitioners can select headings for constructing their own assessment tool. Seen as a whole, it represents an ideal – but the time required to complete it could run into many hours. Some of the questions might be viewed as impertinent by the older British person – such as those relating to 'sexuality' – but the answers could turn out to be very pertinent to the care of some individuals.[3]

Two final points. First, there is some degree of overlap between sections: you will see that activities of daily living, or ADLs, recur in more than one assessment. This is because the sections may be completed by more than one person, as noted above – but it is to be hoped that interviewers will look at the assessment done so far, before going on with it. If there is a discrepancy between the perceptions of, say, the occupational therapist, the nurse and the physiotherapist as to how much someone can do for themselves, then this is valuable in itself. Does the patient or client perform better for one person than another? Is the change due to the passage of time? Or are staff using different assessment criteria?

7

Second, some of the points in the assessment are given as questions, in the second person singular. This does *not* mean that they are intended to be read off the page, but rather that a subjective judgement from the person being assessed is being called for. We cannot stress too much that nothing is engraved in stone – the document is nothing more than a list of pointers and suggestions. How it is used is up to the individual practitioner.

SUBJECTIVE ASSESSMENT WORK SHEET

Section 1   Biographical data base

1.   PATIENT/CLIENT PROFILE

Name: Sex: Marital status:

Address:

Telephone:

Date of birth: Birthplace:

Age at last birthday:

Educational background:

Religion: Ethnic background:

Occupation(s), past and present:

Nearest contact person:

Any other information:

2.   FAMILY PROFILE

Spouse/partner:

Whether living:

(If deceased, give year of death, and cause, if known)

Health status:

8

Age:

Occupation(s):

Children:
(Living: name, sex, age, place of residence)

(Deceased: name, sex, year deceased, cause of death)

Others in household:

Relationship with family and/or significant others:

Any other information:

3. HOME PROFILE
    Type:

    Ownership or rent status:
    Size in relation to need:
    Accessibility to, and mobility within:

    Safety features:
    Management of maintenance and repair:
    Adequacy of heating, lighting, bathroom facilities, etc.:
    Proximity to shops, transport routes, and other amenities:

    Pets and plants:

    Other items of importance to the person (religious objects, hobby materials, etc.):
    Nearest neighbour (if relevant):

    Any other information:

4. COMMUNITY PROFILE

Knowledge of community resources
(e.g. transport, recreation, shopping, health care, church, other [see no. 3]):

Availability of community resources:

Use of community resources:

Accessibility of community resources:

Safety precautions:

Any other information:

5. ECONOMIC PROFILE

Sources of income:

Salary:

Retirement pension:

Occupational pension:

Income support or other State benefit:

Investment income:

Other:

Perception of adequacy:

6. HEALTH AND SOCIAL RESOURCES CURRENTLY USED

GP name   Address and telephone:

Hospital consultant(s)/specialist(s):

Private practitioners (e.g. osteopath, homoeopath or any medical/paramedical professionals):

District nurse: Social worker:

Home help (Social Services/private):

Voluntary worker(s):

Day hospital:

Day centre:

Other:

Section 2   Health perception and management/Cognition and perception/Coping and stress tolerance

1. Perception of current health/well-being

    (**Note:**   A self-rating on a scale from 1 to 10, with 1 being 'never felt worse', to 10 being 'never felt better', may be used here.)

2. Current health status, and understanding of health problems:

    Limitations in ADLs:

    Management of limitations:

    Health goals:

    Other information:

3. Immunisations

   (Include dates of any due within the next year)

4. Allergies (include drugs, foods, contact allergies, and any environmental factors; describe type of reaction):

5. Health examinations:

Examination	Date	Where Done	Findings/Instructions
Physical			
Dental			
Vision			
Hearing			
Breast			
Chest X-ray			
Prostate			
Faecal blood			
Heaf/Mantoux			
Other:			

6. Past health status (serious or chronic illnesses)

Arthritis:	Hepatitis:
Cataracts:	Pneumonia:
Diabetes mellitus:	Seizures:
Glaucoma:	Thyroid problems:
Hearing problems:	Tuberculosis:
Heart disease:	Kidney problems:
Hypertension:	Liver problems:
Peptic ulcer:	Other:

7. Hospitalisations/operations:

Procedure/ condition	Date	Reason	Length of stay

8. Current and recent medication:
(Include: name, dosage, route, frequency, date prescribed (if known), date finished, and the person's understanding of their medications; do not exclude over-the-counter preparations. Note whether or not necessary safety measures are taken, such as carrying steroid medication cards or personal identification and contact numbers.)

9. Relevant family history [See Section 1, no. 2]:
(Include past and present medical conditions; including the person's parents and siblings; draw a family tree, if necessary).

10. Habits with a bearing on health

Smoking

Type:

Quantity:

Duration:

Inhales?:

Relationship to anxiety or stress:

Desire to give up?:

Alcohol

Type(s):

Frequency (expressed as units per day/week):

Relationship to anxiety/stress:

13

Caffeine
Type(s):

Frequency (expressed as cups per day):

Relationships to anxiety/stress:

Other
Methods of lessening stress/relieving boredom
(e.g. hobbies, pursuits and pastimes):

11. Sensory status
    Hearing (all sounds/high frequencies)

    Vision
    Full vision: Colour discrimination:

    Night vision: Depth perception:

    Peripheral vision: Reading:

    Taste

    Smell

    Touch
    Pressure/pain: Temperature:

    Speech

12. Assistive devices
    Hearing aid: Spectacles/contact lenses:
    Other (e.g. induction loop):

13. Cognitive status

    Memory (recent and remote):

    Perceived learning difficulties:

    Mental skills (e.g. crossword puzzles, games):

14. Emotional status

    Self-perception:

    Anxious: Bored: Fearful:

    Depressed: Tense: Suspicious:

    When (if) you have a big problem (any problem) in your life, how do you handle it?

    Do you handle everyday problems as well as most persons your age?

    Interviewer's perception:

    Comments:

15. Client's description of a typical day

Section 3 Nutrition and metabolism/Skin integrity

1. What is your usual daily food and fluid intake?

Meal	Time	Food eaten	Amount (approx.)	Calories (approx.)

    Snacks:

    Total calories (approx.)

2. Special preferences or prescribed restrictions in relation to food/fluid intake:

3. Description of appetite:

4. Companionship during mealtimes:

5. Ability to buy/prepare food:

6. Ability to chew/swallow different types of food:

7. Use of food supplements (e.g. 'Build-Up', 'Complan', vitamins and minerals):

8. Satisfaction with present weight:

9. Self-evaluation of nutritional status:

10. Dyspeptic problems (e.g. indigestion, flatulence, nausea, etc.) – if any of these arise, what precipitates the onset, and what relieves it?

11. Which of the following apply?

Regular use of antacids	Eats slowly
Eats too quickly	Eats crisps, sweets or other snacks
Eats even when not hungry	Always adds salt to food
Is aware of 'healthy eating'	Avoids refined and/or processed foods
Maintains ideal weight within 10lb/5kg	Skips meals
Uses salt/sugar substitutes	Nibbles food all day

12. Skin care practices: skin, nails and hair

    Uses cream or oils: Frequency of bathing:

    Type of soap used:

13. Occurrence of skin lesions, bruises or bleeding:

14. Care of skin lesions:

15. Changes in characteristics or colour of skin, especially extremities:

16. Skin condition:

    Dry: Moist: Pigmentation change:

17. Nail care practices:

    Frequency of cutting:

    Method of cutting:

    Ability to cut own nails:

    Chiropody:

18. Hair care practices:

    Ability to care for hair:

    Changes in hair condition:

    Use of conditioners, dyes or special shampoo, etc.:

    Use of wig:

    Other information:

Section 4   Elimination patterns

1. How often do you pass urine in a 24-hour period?

17

2. Have you ever taken medication that affects your urine?

3. Can you always respond to the urge to void?

4. Do you ever have any problems in this area?

5. Have you ever practiced exercises for bladder/pelvic floor muscles?

6. When do you usually have a bowel movement?

7. Do you use any laxatives? How effective are they?

8. What do you do to help maintain a regular bowel habit?

9. Does anything ever interfere with your usual bowel habit?

10. Do you ever have any problems with passing stool? (Include haemorrhoids, straining, etc.)

Urinalysis:

Other information:

Section 5   Activity – rest patterns/Sleep – rest pattern

1. Describe any social/leisure activities [see Section 2, no. 10]:

2. Is there sufficient energy for you to do all you would like?

3. Self-rating of physical fitness:

4. Mobility status:
(Describe any aids used, the person's ability to use them, and how they feel about them; also include ability to rise from chair, climb stairs, and so on)

5.   Is there any:

    Contracture   Pain on movement

    Paralysis   Spasm

    Amputation   Other limiting factor

(If so, describe location, degree of limitation and any assistive measures required.)

6.   Perceived ability for:

    Feeding: Grooming:

    Bathing: General mobility:

    Independent use of toilet: Cooking:

    Mobility in bed: Home maintenance/
                                  housework:

    Dressing: Shopping:

7.   Circulatory problems – precipitating factors, effects on activity and relief measures

    Chest pain: Tachycardia:

    Oedema: Cramps:

    Other(s):

    Sleep

8.   Type of bed: Sleeps alone?

9.   Usual sleep pattern (include times of going to bed and getting up, times of sleeping – if different – and daytime naps):

10. Practices that help with going to sleep:

11. If you still do not feel rested on awakening, what do you do about it?

Breathing

12. What helps or hinders your breathing?

13. Record any degree of:

Orthopnoea: Dyspnoea:

Shortness of breath: Wheezing:

Cough: Other:

14. Sputum characteristics:

Other information:

Section 6   Self and others/Values and beliefs

(It may be useful to review all the information collected so far, before starting on this section of the assessment.)

1. Do you see as much of your family and friends as you would like?

2. How much time do you have to yourself?

3. Do you ever feel lonely? What do you do about it?

4. Do you feel part of the area where you live? (Note: if the person lives in sheltered accommodation, a council-run home, or something similar, the question should be phrased to focus on how they feel about living there.)

5. Have there been any major changes in your life recently?

6. Is there someone in whom you can confide, and trust?

7. How would you describe yourself, in a few sentences?

8. Describe how you think other people see you.

9. What makes you feel good about yourself?

10. What makes you annoyed or angry? What do you do about it?

11. What sorts of things get you down? What do you do about them?

12. Name three things about yourself that you would *not* like to change.

Comments:

Sexuality

13. Are your needs for affection being met?

14. Female reproductive system factors

Vaginal discharge: Itching:

Lesions: Breast mass:

Nipple discharge: Breast pain:

Mastectomy: Prosthesis:

Breast self-examination: Other:

21

15. Menopausal or post-menopausal problems

16. Use of hormones or other medications related to the reproductive system

17. History of birth control methods and reproductive practices

18. Male reproductive system factors

Scrotal swelling: Lesions:

Discharge: Prostate problems:

Penile/scrotal   Use of condoms for
self-examination: prevention of infectious
                                     diseases

Other:

Values and beliefs:

18. What are your plans for the future?

19. Attitudes towards death and dying

20. Self-description of the importance of religion in life

21. Religious affiliations

Opportunity and ability to attend religious services:

Contact with clergy:

Importance of religious programmes on TV and radio:

Significance of religious holidays, and their observance:

Discussion points

1. How long is 'too long' for an assessment to take?
2. At what point do the important tasks of gathering information and establishing rapport become a counter-productive form-filling exercise?
3. Is it really necessary to consider the older person's 'sexuality' at all?
4. Does a nurse working within the NHS have any need to know about her patients' or clients' financial status?

CHAPTER TWO

The physical changes of ageing and how to assess them

Introductory note

British-trained nurses who take up jobs in the United States are often struck by the extended range of nursing duties that they are expected to undertake – including many which they were previously used to seeing as falling within the domain of medical staff. Physical examination comes into this category.

At the National Ward Sisters' Conference held in London in 1990, Barbara Vaughan, a leading British nurse, gave a lecture on extended roles, entitled 'Extension, Expansion or Extinction?'. In this, she looked at the increasing number of 'medical' tasks that were falling into the category of 'nursing duties (extended role)', such as giving intravenous drugs, and drew a clear distinction between what she differentiated as 'extended' and 'expanded' roles. In the former, the nurse is taking on tasks previously undertaken by medical staff because it is often more convenient for her to do so: it is quicker and easier for her to catheterise a male patient, or give an intravenous (IV) antibiotic, than to ring round trying to find a doctor who can do it; and it is, of course, of benefit to the patient, who receives treatment that much more promptly. This sort of extension has been welcomed in the health service, by and large, because it is so cost-effective.

Expanded roles are another matter. In this case, the nurse takes responsibility for certain tasks because she is better trained to do them than anyone else. One example of this is nurse prescription, where a suitably qualified and experienced nurse, who has much more contact with her patients than the medical staff can ever hope to have, might be in the best position to assess a person's degree of pain and prescribe the most effective available analgesia. Unlike extended roles, expansion is not always looked on favourably by senior medical and nursing staff, for reasons which are too complex to go into here.

Vaughan's final category, 'extinction', comes when nurses are so busy doing the work of medical staff, they are left with no time to nurse – thus enabling the holders of the purse strings to say 'why have expensive, trained nurses at all, when the care is being delivered so well by cheap, untrained staff?'

This may not seem to have much to do with physical assessment of the older person; but the following chapter is made up of a suggested guide to the subject for North American practitioners, and a great deal of what is described bears little relation to the sorts of things that most of us in Britain actually do in this area. This is the kind of examination that is normally carried out by housemen or senior house officers on the patient's admission to hospital, or by the general practitioner in the domestic or nursing home setting. However, it has been retained for the UK edition because firstly, it is very comprehensive, and serves as a good guide to the anatomy and physiology that underlies successful care planning for physical problems; and secondly, it is a good indication of the sorts of skills that we in this country may one day have to develop. (Any reader who would like to know more about the sorts of assessment skills expected of the North American nurse will find them detailed in a small book by Morton.)[1]

The only amendments are small ones in terminology, and some references have been supplemented or replaced with others that may be easier to locate in a British nursing library. (**Note**: As this book was being prepared for publication, the UKCC published *The Scope of Professional Practice*, which effectively ends the need for extended role certification. It will be some time, however, before the effects of this ruling are felt.)

* * *

In the United States, various licensing regulations require that a physical examination be completed and recorded by a physician within a given time period associated with the admission to acute and long-term care facilities. The nurse needs to review the findings and note any parts of it that have been deferred. Therefore, it may not be necessary for the nurse to perform a complete physical examination initially. In the home health setting, it is also necessary to have a statement of health.

The physical assessment performed by the nurse may be very lengthy and thorough or may focus only on the principal problem and general condition of the person. The purposes of the assessment are to further enhance communication and rapport and to obtain baseline information about the health status of the older person. The assessment must not be hurried; the procedure must be explained, privacy must be maintained, and the environment kept sufficiently warm to protect the person from chilling.

The following material discusses normal age changes commonly manifested in older persons. These normal age changes are addressed in the basic strategies of the physical assessment, which are inspection, palpation, percussion and auscultation. *Inspection* involves the systematic observation of the body through the special senses of sight, hearing, smell, and touch. Eliopoulos[2] pointed out that a great deal can be assessed through odours emitted from the client. Excessive use of perfumes can be associated with poor sense of smell, breath odour may indicate lung abscesses and infections in the mouth, and an odour of newly-mown clover may indicate liver failure. *Palpation* involves touching the body surfaces with the hands or fingers to identify temperature, texture, organ location and size. *Percussion* is the tapping of specific body areas to determine information about underlying tissue. *Auscultation* involves listening to body sounds with a stethoscope. The evaluation of the various organ systems may be done in any order.

Head and neck

It is usually most convenient to begin the physical assessment with the evaluation of the head and neck. The head is inspected for gross lesions and asymmetry. Visual acuity decreases with advancing age. Peripheral vision and colour vision decrease. The warm colours such as orange and yellow can be seen better than blues and greens. There is increased sensitivity to glare, and increased adjustment time to changes in light sensitivities. The eyes are observed for swelling, redness, increased tear production or dryness. The eyelids are observed for lesions and encrustations. The iris of the eye is inspected for the presence/absence of an arcus senilis, a whitish ring around the cornea. The size of the pupils is noted. The pupillary reaction to light can be evaluated with a pen torch. Vision may be checked by asking the person to read printed material or to describe a picture or article on a wall. Cataracts can be identified by shining the pen torch at a 45° angle to the eye. Cloudy opacities are seen if cataracts are present. A fundoscopic examination may be performed if the nurse has the necessary skills and equipment.

Major changes in hearing include reduced perception of high frequency tones. It becomes more difficult to discriminate sounds when there is more than one sound being received. Cerumen (ear wax) becomes more viscous.[3]

26

The external ears are inspected for symmetry, lesions and any obvious drainage. The lower lobe should be observed for a longitudinal fold, which may indicate cardiovascular disease. The internal ear may be examined with an auroscope; a cone of light should be seen on the eardrum. The ear canal should be inspected for accumulations of impacted cerumen and scarring from previous infections, which may cause hearing loss.

Hearing is tested by standing behind the person, pronouncing two-syllable words, and asking the person to repeat the words as they are enunciated. If the person uses a hearing aid, the hearing should be assessed both with and without its being in place.

The Weber and Rinne tests may also be performed. The Weber test is done by striking a tuning fork and then pressing the stem of the fork against the skull in the centre of the head. The sound should be heard equally in both ears; the person is asked whether it is louder on one side in comparison to the other.

The Rinne test is done by striking a tuning fork and then placing the stem of the fork on the mastoid bone. When the person can no longer hear the sound, the fork is placed near the auditory meatus. The sound should again be heard. Normally air conduction (AC) is greater than bone conduction (BC); this is expressed as AC > BC. The older adult will frequently have some hearing loss, most commonly due to presbycusis, which is a loss due to changes in the inner ear structure.

The nose and nostrils are observed for obvious deviation and drainage. The ability to smell is tested by asking the person to identify the smell of an alcohol swab, or a similarly pungent odour, while the eyes are closed. A decline in the ability to smell occurs with ageing.

In the oral cavity of an older person, the teeth become worn as a result of abrasions of the enamel and dentin. There is decreased production of saliva, and shrinkage of the gums. Both incidence and severity of periodontal disease rise with age; it is the most usual cause of tooth loss.[4] The oral cavity is carefully inspected for dentition and condition of the mucosa. Any foul odours are noted, since breath odour can indicate various health problems. If the person has dentures, they are observed for proper fit, cleanliness and occlusion. The gums and periodontal tissue are examined for colour, moisture, presence/absence of lesions and infections. Any teeth which are broken or in poor repair, are noted, as well as the general state of dental hygiene.

27

The entire head and neck are gently palpated for tenderness, sores, and enlarged nodes. The thyroid gland, which is located across the trachea below the cricoid cartilage, is also palpated; this is often made easier if the person is asked to swallow.

Skin/integument

Loss of subcutaneous fat and elasticity resulting in wrinkling of the skin occurs with advancing age. Sweat glands decrease in activity and number. Sometimes pigment cells hypertrophy, causing hyperpigmentation or 'liver spots'. Blood supply to the skin is affected as capillaries become more fragile, due to the loss of supporting subcutaneous fat. Hair thins and hair roots atrophy. The nails become thicker and more brittle, and their growth is slowed.

The skin is observed for colour, presence or absence of lesions, moisture and/or dryness. The frequency of cherry angiomas increase with ageing, but the significance of this phenomenon is not known. The nails are observed for evidence of clubbing, discoloration and splitting. The skin and nails are also observed for general cleanliness and odour. The breasts are inspected for symmetry, dimpling and inversion of the nipples, which may signify breast pathology.

The skin is also assessed by gentle touch for temperature, texture and turgor. Turgor is best measured by gently raising or moving the skin of the forehead and observing how rapidly the crease disappears or returns to normal. Any lesions should be described in terms of size, determined by simple measurement if the shape is regular, or by using a tracing if not; colour; presence or absence of hair; induration; and pain or numbness. Special attention must be paid to the feet. They should be carefully inspected for any lesions, especially in the areas between the toes. The examiner must also record any corns, callouses, ulcers, warts, bunions or hammer-toe deviations. The toenails are observed for cleanliness, colour, abnormal thickening or fungal infections.

Respiratory system

The respiratory system undergoes the greatest age-associated change and decrease in function, even though lung tissue regenerates well. Stretch and muscle tone of the chest wall decrease, as do all the muscles associated with respiration. The ribs become less mobile, and the costal cartilage calcifies. There is decreased action of the cilia, dilation of the bronchioles, and a decrease in the number of alveoli. (The alveolar surface area, which is about $75m^2$ at the age of 30, decreases by approximately 4 per cent per decade from then on.[5]) The cough reflex and cough effectiveness are reduced. These changes result in reduced depth of respiration, decreased ventilation, and decreased vital capacity, which some researchers believe to be an accurate predictor of the general health of older persons[6]. These changes result in reduced oxygenation of all body tissues. When interpreting arterial blood gas (ABG) values, 1mm Hg for every year of age over 60 to age 90 should be subtracted from the PaO value.[7]

Inspection of the respiratory system should be done with the person seated in a chair, to observe whether there is symmetrical chest expansion. The shape of the chest, any skeletal deformities, and respiratory effort are observed.

The index and third fingers are run along the spinal column to determine any abnormal curvature. Diaphragmatic excursion is evaluated by grasping the rib cage with both hands, with the thumbs at the level of the 10th ribs near the spine. The movement of the thumbs is observed while the person inhales deeply; this movement should be equal and symmetrical. Tactile fremitus is evaluated by placing the side or palm of the dominant hand at the right scapular area, and asking the person to say '99'. The hand is then moved to the left scapular area and progressively down the back, alternating sides. The person repeats '99' each time the hand is moved. The vibrations palpated should feel equal.

Percussion should always be done very gently. The entire posterior chest is percussed, except the scapular areas where bony structures overlie lung tissue. Resonance should be equal on both sides of the chest. The flat large diaphragm of the stethoscope is used to listen to the lungs while the person breathes deeply with the mouth open. The auscultation must be done slowly, to avoid hyperventilation. The lungs should sound clear, with no adventitious or abnormal sounds. *Rales* sound like a lock of hair rubbed between the fingers, near the ear; *rhonchi* are continuous deeper sounds caused by obstruction to the air flow; and *wheezes* are high-pitched whistling sounds caused by partial airway obstruction.

Cardiovascular system

The respiratory and cardiovascular systems are closely related; a change in one system directly affects the other. The heart muscle becomes stiffer and less compliant with age. Increased rigidity and thickening occur in the heart valves, and efficiency of blood return to the heart decreases. The aorta becomes less elastic as it enlarges and elongates, and coronary circulation decreases. Systolic blood pressure generally rises with time until age 64, and then declines; the heart returns to its resting rate more slowly after exercise, and rates exceeding 120 beats per minute are poorly tolerated.[8]

The anterior chest is observed for any obvious deformities, lesions or pulsations. The ball of the hand is used first to locate the point of maximum impulse (PMI) or the apex of the heart. This should be located at the fifth intercostal space in the midclavicular line. Percussion is not generally performed in the physical assessment of the heart; however, this technique may be useful for defining the borders of an enlarged heart.

The large flat diaphragm is first used to listen to the heart sounds. Beginning at the PMI, the stethoscope is gradually moved up the chest, to the left of the sternum. The first and second heart sounds (S_1 and S_2) are first identified. S_1 is the louder sound at the PMI. S_2 is the louder sound at the top of the heart. The sounds should be of equal intensity at Erb's point, or the third left intercostal space. The sounds are evaluated for rate, rhythm and intensity. There should be no extra sounds, though a 'splitting' of the S_2 is considered to be normal on inspiration. Identification and evaluation of heart sounds is dependent upon the skills and experience of the assessor. The physician must be notified if murmurs or extracardiac sounds are heard; murmurs are best heard with the smaller bell of the stethoscope, which must be well sealed against the skin surface. Data from phonocardiographic studies show that murmurs are present in 60 per cent or more of older clients; the most common type is a soft systolic ejection murmur heard at the base of the heart.[9]

The blood pressure is taken in both arms, seated, standing and lying; a variation of 10mm Hg from arm to arm is considered normal.[10] Serial blood pressures should be taken if there are known cardiovascular problems, or if the person is taking medication for hypertension. (There is currently much debate about what constitutes 'hypertension', but many researchers have accepted the World Health Organisation's statement that 160/95mm Hg is the upper limit of 'normal' blood pressure.[11])

The carotid arteries are gently palpated individually. The diaphragm of the stethoscope is gently placed on the carotid artery to determine the presence or absence of *bruits* (abnormal sounds caused by impeded blood flow). The jugular veins are observed for distension, preferably with the head of the bed or examining table raised at a 45° angle. The peripheral pulses (radial, brachial, femoral, popliteal, dorsalis pedis, and posterior tibialis) are evaluated for presence/absence, quality, and intensity. The apical pulse is compared with the radial pulse rate.

Abdomen

The principal age-related changes in the stomach, small intestine and colon are decreased motility and peristalsis. There is a decrease in the production of gastrointestinal secretions, and a delay in emptying time of the stomach. There is also a decrease in the number of cells on the absorbing surfaces of the small intestine. The liver becomes smaller and there are decreases in weight and hepatic blood flow. Liver function declines with age. The gallbladder has a slower emptying time, and the bile becomes thicker and has less volume.

The usual order of inspection, palpation, auscultation and percussion is altered in the assessment of the abdomen: the sequence is inspection, auscultation, percussion and palpation. The abdomen is inspected for symmetry and abnormalities of contour which could indicate obstruction, hernia or tumour. Arterial pulsations also may be noted. Any scars, striae or dilated veins are recorded.

The diaphragm of the stethoscope is placed lightly on the abdomen, and all quadrants are auscultated. Bowel sounds should be present throughout the abdomen; an absence is a medical emergency, and for this reason, it is strongly suggested that the *minimum* time for this procedure should be five minutes.

The size of the liver and spleen and the location of the stomach can be determined by percussing the abdomen. Percussion is begun upward on the right side to identify the border of the liver. The sound elicited changes from tympany to dullness over the liver. The stomach is usually located slightly to the left of the midline in the area of the ribcage. The spleen can be palpated in the area of the 10th rib on the left side.

Palpation of all four quadrants of the abdomen is done lightly with the fingertips. Light palpation is done to identify masses, tenderness, and location of abdominal organs. If the person complains of any pain or tenderness, palpation should not be done. The authors recommend that only light to moderate palpation be performed, due to potential for injury to underlying structures.

31

Musculoskeletal system

The number of muscle cells and elastic tissue decreases with the ageing process. The skeletal muscles atrophy, and strength and size decrease. Cartilage tissue thins and tends to yellow. The joints become less mobile. Changes occur in the vertebral column, which result in decreased height. Bone mass decreases and demineralises, resulting in bones becoming brittle. The older client will have decreased muscle size as muscle mass declines with ageing.[12]

The person's gait is observed for limps, hemiparesis and other abnormalities. The shoes should be examined for excessive wear on the heels, which can indicate a gait disturbance. The person's ability to sit and rise from a chair is also observed. The limbs are measured for equality of length and girth to establish baseline data. Muscle strength and integrity are assessed by having the person perform the following movements:

1. squeeze the examiner's hands;
2. shrug the shoulders against the force of the examiner's hands;
3. flex the knees and push against the examiner's hands with the feet.

Range of motion is also evaluated.

The hands are examined for the presence of Heberden's and Bouchard's nodes, and Dupuytren's contractures. Heberden's nodes are hardened areas on the dorsal surfaces of the distal joints of the fingers, whilst Bouchard's nodes are located at the proximal joints; the presence of either suggests arthritis. Dupuytren's contractures ('scrivener's palm') involve nodular thickening on the palm of the hand, with the fingers being pulled inwards, severely limiting extension. This is most common amongst people who are diabetic.

The joints are palpated for crepitus, which feels like 'crackling' within the joint. Only light pressure should be used, to avoid causing pain.

Some kyphosis (exaggeration of the curve of the vertebral column) may occur with ageing, most commonly in women — hence the description, 'dowager's hump'.

Neurological system

The brain declines in size and weight with advancing age. A nonfunctional substance, called amyloid, increases. Neurotransmitters decrease, resulting in slowing of the reflexes. There is a decreased ability to respond to multiple stimuli. The number of neurons decreases, but the length of the dendrites increases.[13]

Intelligence and the ability to learn do not decrease, although more time may be required for processing information. Memory remains intact, although in some people, short-term memory may decline with advancing age.[14, 15] The neurological assessment may be initiated by observing the level of consciousness and general demeanour. A mental status examination should be performed at some point. (Researchers in Britain have found it very difficult to estimate the incidence of affective disorders amongst the elderly,[16] but in the United States, emotional illness has been calculated to affect 20 per cent of older adults, and 40 per cent of older adults with physical illnessess.[17] Numerous tools of varying complexity have been devised for this assessment; a comprehensive list is given by Goudie in a recent text.)[18] The chief components of a brief mental status questionnaire (MSQ) are testing of recent and remote memory, orientation, calculation, consciousness, and graphic ability. The following questions can be asked:

1. (Nurse) My name is _____.
2. What is your name?
3. Who is your doctor?
4. Do you know where you are?
5. How old are you?
6. When is your birthday?
7. Where do you live?
8. Who do you live with?
9. Do you remember what my name is?

(British nurses will note the similarity of the MSQ to the Abbreviated Mental Test Score (AMTS), widely used by geriatricians in this country.)

Graphic ability can be assessed by asking the person to write his or her name. The ability to calculate can be assessed by the use of mathematical flash cards or playing cards. This assessment can also serve as a vision check.

The nurse should pay special attention to the person's speech: any unusual slowness, lack of nouns, repetition of words or phrases, stuttering or inappropriate responses should be noted.

The integrity of the cranial nerves (CN) may be assessed. However, the nurse must remember that age-related changes can result in a slowing of the responses.

33

To assess cranial nerve I (CNI), the olfactory nerve, the examiner holds a piece of scented material such as an alcohol swab, testing one nostril at a time whilst compressing the other. Detection of the correct odour is, obviously, the 'correct' response, but it is normal for the sense of smell to become less acute with ageing.

CN II, the optic nerve, is concerned with visual fields and acuity; a description of how these are tested has already been given (page 33). There is often little point in examining nerves controlling the eye muscles (CN III, IV and VI: oculomotor, trochlear and abducens) because of the normal age-related loss of convergence ability, and past surgical procedures such as cataract extraction may have an influence on the appearance and reaction time of the eye.

The integrity of the trigeminal and facial nerves (CN V and VII) is tested by asking the person to frown, clench the teeth, show the teeth by raising the upper lip, tightly close the eyes, make chewing movements of the jaw, and puff the cheeks and smile.

The branch of the facial nerve that exits just anterior to the tragus of the ear can be gently tapped to elicit Chvostek's sign. A positive response is a facial tremor, and can indicate hypocalcaemia.

The snout reflex of Wartenburg, or pouting reflex, if present, is indicative of diffuse cerebral dysfunction.[19] It is elicited by applying brief pressure to the lips, a positive response being puckering.

The acoustic nerve, CN VIII, is tested as described on page 38.

CN IX, the glossopharyngeal, is tested by touching the tonsillar area very lightly with a cotton tipped applicator; the nerve is intact if the person gags. At the same time, the integrity of the vagus nerve (CN X) can be evaluated by observing any uvular deviation.

The spinal accessory nerve (CN XI) can be checked by asking the person to shrug his or her shoulders; a lag on one side and inability to resist downward pressure from the examiner's hands on the shoulders is abnormal (see Musculoskeletal system, above).

Finally, the hypoglossal nerve (CN XII) is evaluated by asking the person to stick out the tongue; there should be no deviation.

Great care must be taken when evaluating deep tendon reflexes, as there is a possibility of causing pain in, or injury to, arthritic joints. The Babinski sign is elicited by lightly stroking the lateral aspect of the sole of the foot from heel to ball, and across the ball. A positive response, which is indicative of upper motor neuron paralysis, is dorsiflexion and fanning of the toes. The older person will have decreased strength of reflexes in general, but it should be possible to elicit all of them.[20]

A convenient method of evaluating sensation (or lack of it) in the various areas of the body is through the use of a tuning fork, or other vibrating device. This is placed over different parts of the body's surface, including the major joints, and the person is asked to report when the vibration is first perceived; it is sometimes useful to do this test twice, once with the person's eyes open, and again with them closed.

Genitourinary system

The kidneys are primarily responsible for the regulation of fluid volume and soluble solids in the body. It is known that shifts in body composition occur with age; water content decreases, while fat concentration increases. Kidneys decrease in size and lose the ability to concentrate urine efficiently, especially at night. There is reduced bladder capacity and loss of muscle tone, and the bladder may fail to empty completely on urination. In men, the prostate gland undergoes many changes, the most common of which is increase in size; this may be benign or malignant.[21]

Sexual desire, capability, and functioning remain intact throughout the life span of healthy adults. Among females, the menses and ovulation cease with menopause; the ovaries and uterus decrease in size, whilst the vagina becomes thinner and less elastic, lubrication is decreased, and vaginal secretions become more alkaline.

Among men, sperm production continues throughout life, but the number of sperm and their motility decline; the size and firmness of the testes also decrease.[22] It takes longer for an older male to achieve an erection and reach climax, and the total volume of ejaculate is reduced.

Internal pelvic examination of the female, and prostatic examination of the male, are tasks usually carried out by the physician.[23]

Endocrine system

Hormone secretion decreases with advancing age, and this has widespread effects on the whole body; and in addition to this, the tissues' ability to respond to hormones also decreases. An example of this is the way that some older people's cells become unable to utilise insulin efficiently, even though plasma levels of the hormone seem adequate.[24] Changes also appear in the immune system, resulting in a slowing of repair to damaged tissues. Production of antibodies and lymphocytes decline, causing increased susceptibility to disease. Much research is being carried on in this area, with hope that some of the degenerative changes of ageing will become better understood.

Many physiological changes occur as a natural part of the ageing process in all living things, from the amoeba to man – possibly the most sophisticated and most cellularly differentiated organism. Humans have tried throughout history to define and describe the processes of cellular ageing, and many theories have been proposed – but as yet, there is no definitive answer.[25]

At the cellular level, the most outstanding age-related change is the accumulation of a pigment called lipofuscin. This is a brownish substance, often referred to as 'age pigment' – but its effect on the body's physiology is not understood. It does not accumulate in all tissues, but it is commonly found in neural, muscle, liver, spleen, heart, adrenal and pancreatic tissue.[26]

For physiological purposes, ageing can be defined as the loss of function of cells or their inability to replace themselves. Another definition is a diminished ability to respond to stress. It is not completely clear which changes are the result of a disease process, and which are inherent parts of the ageing process; so the question is, does disease cause ageing, or does ageing cause disease?

* * *

A suggested physical assessment worksheet is provided on the following pages.

PHYSICAL ASSESSMENT WORKSHEET

A. GENERAL SURVEY

Height: Weight (recent changes):

Vital signs:
Blood pressure (sitting, standing, lying):

Temperature:
Heart rate:
Respiration:

General appearance:

B. INTEGUMENTARY SYSTEM

Colour: Rashes:
Moisture:
Texture:
Temperature: Discoloration:
Turgor:

Hair:
  Thickness:
  Texture:
  Lubrication:

Scalp:
  Contour:
  Lesions:

Nails:
  Thickness:
  Circulation:

C   HEAD AND NECK

Head:
  Size:
  Shape:
  Contour:

Face:
  Temporal and masseter muscles (CN V, VII):
  Sinus area:
    Frontal:
    Paranasal:
    Maxillary:

Eyes:
  Visual acuity (CN II):

  Visual field:

  Extraocular movements (CN III, IV ,VI):

  External eye structures:

Pupils:
  Pupillary reflex (CN II):
  Direct and consensual:
  Pupillary accommodation:

Internal eye structure:
  Red reflex:

Ears:
  External ear structure:

  Middle ear structure:
    Tympanic membrane:

  Hearing acuity (CN VIII):
    Rinne test:
    Weber test:

Nose:
  Patency:

  Olfactory sense (CN I):

  Asymmetry:

  Inflammation:

  Deformity:

  Mucosa:
    Colour:
    Lesions:
    Discharge:
    Swelling:
    Evidence of bleeding:

  Septum:
    Deviation:
    Lesion:

    Superficial blood vessels:

Oral cavity:
  Colour:

  Texture:

  Hydration:

Contour:

Lesions:

Mouth odour:

Teeth:
  Number:
  Status: Dentures:

Palate and uvula (CN IX, X):

Tongue (CN XII):

Pharynx:
  Infection, inflammation, lesions:

Neck:
  General structure:

  Trachea:

  Thyroid:
    Masses (size, shape, tenderness, consistency, mobility):

  Muscles (CN XI):

  Shoulder shrug:

  Lymph nodes:

D. LUNGS

  A–P diameter:

  Chest wall (anteriorly, posteriorly, laterally):
    Contour:

  Deformities:

  Retraction:

  Bulging of intercostal spaces:

  Movement during respiration:

  Percussion:

  Lung sounds:

Fremitus:

Diaphragmatic excursion: R _____ cm
                            L _____ cm

E. CARDIOVASCULAR

Pulses (rate and rhythm, amplitude – 0 to + 3):
Apical:
Radial:
Carotid pulse:
Brachial:
Femoral:
Popliteal:
Dorsalis pedis:
Posterior tibial:
Jugular vein:
Heart sounds:
PMI:

F. BREASTS

Size:

Symmetry:

Colour:

Retraction, flattening, contour:

Nipples:

Nodes:

G. ABDOMEN

Shape:

Symmetry:

Movement:

Umbilicus:

Bowel sounds:
Intestinal motility:
Vascular sounds:

Liver:
Midclavicular liver span:

H. FEMALE REPRODUCTIVE

Discharge, itching, burning:

I. MALE REPRODUCTIVE

Discharge, itching, burning:

J. RECTUM

Haemorrhoids:

K. MUSCULOSKELETAL

Range of movements:

Gait:

Posture:

Deformity:

Stiffness or instability of joints:

L. SPINE:

Contour, position, motion:

M. FEET

Skin lesions:
Callous(es):   Fissures between toes:

Corn(s):   Redness:

Oedema: Temperature:

Toenails:
Thickened:
Ingrown:
Overgrown:

N. NEUROLOGICAL

Sensory:
Pain:

Tactile:

Temperature:

Vibration:

Position change stimuli:

Motor function: Co-ordination:
Upper extremities

Lower extremities:

Romberg sign:

Cranial nerve summary (I – XII)

Reflexes:
(0: absent, 1: decreased, 2: normal, 3: increased,
4: spasticity)

Brachioradialis:

Biceps:

Triceps:

Abdominal scratch:

Patellar:

Plantar:

Achilles:

© Brian Booth/The Macmillan Press 1993. Carroll, Brue and Booth,
Caring for Older People: A Nurse's Guide

Discussion points

1. Would the nurse be the best person to perform physical assessments on her patients/clients?
2. Is the standard of physical assessment, as currently performed by hospital doctors and GPs, high enough?

PART II

Actual or potential health problems of older people

Introduction

The elderly are often afflicted with numerous health problems that make assessment difficult. Because of the 'normal' changes outlined in the previous section, older persons, especially those who are debilitated, are more likely to develop health problems than those who are younger. Furthermore, acute illnesses may be manifested differently in older persons, and the onset may not be detected. For example, fever is not a frequent early symptom of respiratory infection in the older person, and many of the elderly experience heart attacks without chest pain – the so-called 'silent MI'. Older persons, as well as caregivers, may ignore 'aches and pains', seeing them as a normal, even expected, part of the ageing process.

Additionally, older persons frequently take numerous medications that may mask or confuse symptoms of disease, or even themselves be the cause of problems. In the following chapters, various health problems and disease processes that commonly affect the elderly are discussed.

Before reading on, however, some nurses may wish to know more about the concept of 'nursing diagnosis', which at the time of writing is not yet widely familiar to the profession in the United Kingdom. This is not the place to discuss the arguments about whether or not the idea should be adopted in this country[1]; what follows is intended to be an introduction to the subject for readers who have yet to encounter it, to help explain the thinking behind the suggested interventions that appear in the following chapters. Nurses who are familiar with the subject may wish to skip the next section.

Nursing diagnosis

Diagnosis – from the Greek *dia* (through) and *gnosis* (an enquiry) – is an excellent word for describing the process in which we, as nurses, amass the information on which we build our plans of care. However, in most people's minds, it is inextricably bound up with medicine and ill-health.

Many writers on nursing have tried, at various times, to reclaim the term for our profession. These are just a few examples:

Diagnosis is an investigative operation that enables nurses to make judgements about the existing health-care situation and decisions about what can and should be done.[2]

A nursing diagnosis is a description of the individual patient's condition as a total human being; it includes physiological, psychological, social, economic and spiritual aspects of his life.[3]

A clear statement of the patient's problems, as ascertained from the nursing assessment, is increasingly being referred to as a nursing diagnosis.[4]

Nursing diagnosis as a critical component of the nursing process . . . is a convenient, logical way to reference nursing standards.[5]

Although nursing diagnoses and medical diagnoses are 'independent' of each other, they are interrelated, and should not be considered in isolation from one another.[6]

It may seem that there is nothing new in any of this – and indeed, the idea is over forty years old – and the difference between 'assessment' and 'diagnosis' may seem to be purely semantic. But this is not the case.

Nursing diagnoses are component parts of a *taxonomy*, or classification system. One taxonomy with which nurses are familiar is the one that breaks human function down into *systems*: nervous, respiratory and so on. The taxonomy of nursing diagnosis is based on the idea that there are recognisable clusters of signs, symptoms and behaviour that can be identified on assessment. If these can be classified in a similar way to medical diagnoses, pro-diagnosis theorists would argue, then information can become more specific and more objective.

For example, a phrase that elderly care nurses are used to seeing is 'loss of mobility' – but what does it mean, exactly? That is left to the individual to decide, at the moment, but a North American nurse using the Omaha VNA/PCS taxonomy[7] would turn to the section on neuromuscularskeletal function, where she could select one of the following as a starting point: limited range of motion, decreased muscle strength, decreased coordination/balance, decreased muscle tone, decreased sensation, increased sensation, gait/ambulation disturbance, difficulty managing activities of daily living, tremors/ seizure, or even 'other'.[8]

In this example, it can be seen that the assessing nurse must be more specific than might otherwise be the case. This in turn leads, eventually, to an ability to compare like with like, when discussing care in more general terms; if someone proposes nursing interventions for specific diagnostic categories, the removal of ambiguous terms should enable the audience to understand exactly what the proposer has in mind. (In this book, the authors are using the NANDA taxonomy.)

It is still too soon to say whether nursing diagnoses will find a place in British nursing practice; the arguments on both sides are not yet fully developed, but it looks as though there will be some lively debate in the future. Any reader who wishes to look deeper into the subject has a wealth of sources to choose from, but at the time of writing all the major texts appear to be by North American authors.[9]

CHAPTER THREE

Respiratory problems

Common health problems of the respiratory system of the older adult can be related to the characteristic changes that occur. The thorax becomes stiffer, lungs less elastic, and expansion of the rib cage more limited, resulting in lungs that are poorly aerated. As a result of structural changes, vital capacity decreases as residual volume increases, resulting in an alteration in the exchange of gases in the lungs. Common health problems of the older person include pneumonia, emphysema and tuberculosis. The purpose of this chapter is to guide the nurse in careful analysis of the data obtained, so that she can formulate valid nursing diagnoses with appropriate nursing interventions for clients with health problems of the respiratory system.

Pneumonia

Pneumonia is inflammation of the lungs caused by bacteria, viruses, chemicals or allergens. The elderly and debilitated are more susceptible to pneumonia due to declines in respiratory function, which include less effective coughing, and changes in the immune system. Fever and pleuritic pain are often absent; confusion and restlessness may be the only symptoms. Older people are at serious risk from influenza; the over-65s, while making up only 10 per cent of the number infected, account for 80 per cent of the deaths related to it.[1] However, there is much disagreement amongst experts on the value of immunisation, although the majority seems to be coming down in favour of it for the 'at risk' elderly.[2] Pneumococcal vaccine is likely to remain a subject of debate for some time.

Examples of potential nursing diagnoses

1 Ineffective airway clearance due to tenacious secretions.
2 Impaired gas exchange due to ventilation – perfusion imbalance.

3 Alteration in nutrition (less than body requirements) due to loss of appetite, fatigue.
4 Decreased activity tolerance due to fatigue.
5 Sleep pattern disturbance due to coughing.
6 Alteration in comfort due to pleuritic pain.
7 Potential for impairment of skin integrity due to immobility.
8 Alteration in bowel elimination, constipation, due to immobility.

Potential nursing interventions

1 and 2   Improve airway clearance and gas exchange.

- Position in the semi- or high- side-lying position, if the person cannot assume or maintain the position for postural drainage.
- Support the chest with small pillows or a bath blanket.
- Maximise coughing effort by teaching/assisting the person to take a deep breath, breathe again, and cough on the second exhalation.
- Maintain adequate humidity, to prevent drying of secretions, through the use of a continuous vaporiser/warm air humidifier. If this equipment is unavailable, it may be possible to improvise a substitute by placing bowls of water on room heating sources, if it is safe to do so, or the person could be taken to a high humidity area (such as a bathroom) for periods.
- Auscultate the lung field frequently for the presence of adventitious sounds and effectiveness of airway clearance.
- Use suction only when necessary to maintain patency of the airway; if possible, pre-oxygenate beforehand. Remember not to apply suction when inserting the catheter, do not exceed 15 seconds, and allow the person time to recover from this potentially distressing procedure.

Nursing consideration   Suctioning can damage airway tissues, and can also lead to anoxia; it is also a source of entry for secondary infection. It is a skilled procedure, which must never be undertaken by nurses who have not received thorough training in technique.

3   Maintain adequate nutrition for body requirements.

- Encourage a fluid intake of at least 1500–2000 ml/day, if it can be tolerated, and is not contraindicated by other conditions such as congestive cardiac failure or renal impairment.

51

- Monitor and record intake and output.
- Provide frequent small meals, rather than large ones at long intervals, and assist with feeding as necessary.
- Administer or assist with oral hygiene at frequent, recorded intervals, and keep a supply of ice on hand to prevent drying-out of the mucous membranes.

4-5 Conserve body resources to increase activity tolerance and allow for adequate sleep and rest.

- Plan necessary procedures and activities to allow for a resting period for the patient between each.
- Do not allow institutional schedules (for example, meal times, medication times) to over-ride the individual's needs.
- Check whether procedures/activities that have been suggested for the patient are really essential, or whether they could be deferred until he is better able to tolerate them (for example, hair washing).

6 Relieve discomfort due to pleuritic pain.

- Give prescribed analgesia, whenever possible before pain occurs.
- Support the chest and maximise coughing effort as described in item 1, above.

7 Implement pressure area care.

- Ensure that the person's position is changed at least two-hourly, and that pressure areas are checked at the same time for their condition.
- Use pressure-relieving cushions and/or mattresses, if the person is deemed to be 'at risk' by pressure-sore risk calculation.

8 Prevent constipation.

- Monitor fluid intake (see item 3, above).
- Establish what the person's normal bowel habit is, and plan accordingly.
- Add bran to the diet (consult dietition for recommendations about quantity) and, if liked, whole-fruit juices.
- Ensure that the person is in the most upright position possible for toileting; if activity tolerance permits, a toilet cubicle provides more privacy than a bedpan or bedside commode.

Emphysema

Emphysema occurs when the alveoli of the lungs are distended or ruptured. There is an accompanying loss of lung elasticity. The symptoms are slow in onset and resemble normal age-related changes in the respiratory system. Weakness, weight loss and loss of appetite are common symptoms; restlessness and dyspnoea develop later in the disease.

Examples of potential nursing diagnoses

Diagnostic statements include those listed in the discussion on pneumonia, above. 'Anxiety, severe, related to ineffective breathing' and 'knowledge deficit, use of medication' are others to consider when planning the care of the person with emphysema.

Potential nursing interventions

1 Improve airway clearance and gas exchange:

- Teach breathing exercises, including 'pursed-lip' breathing; this involves having the person inhale slowly and deeply whilst the lips are pursed, as if to whistle.
- Encourage coughing with short 'huffs', rather than sustained coughing action.
- Administer and monitor oxygen therapy as prescribed.

Nursing consideration The rate of oxygen administration should never exceed 24–28 per cent, to avoid overriding the brain's triggering mechanism for breathing. The nurse must be vigilant for signs of hypoxia, which include:

- Increased pulse rate
- Restlessness
- Flaring of the nostrils
- Intercostal and sternal retractions; and
- Disorientation.

Nasal hygiene needs to be kept in mind during oxygen therapy, as the membranes will rapidly become dry. If the patient is able to blow his own nose from time to time, this may be sufficient; if not, it will be necessary to clean the membranes with a moistened cotton bud, and possibly, to apply a lubricant – sparingly.

2 Conserve body resources to increase activity tolerance and allow for adequate rest and sleep.

- Allow the person to find his own position of greatest comfort. He or she is often more comfortable in a chair, recliner or, when in bed, in a fairly high sitting position.
- Keep the room environment as cool as possible.
- Use an over-bed table for the person to lean over whilst in bed or in a chair (the 'orthopnoeic position').

3 Reduce anxiety.

- Have the anxious and/or dyspnoeic person concentrate on the nurse's breathing pattern, using the pursed-lip technique and appearing as relaxed as possible.
- Relaxation training may be very helpful in relieving anxiety for the person who is having difficulty breathing.[4]

4 Teach the correct way to use inhalers and nebulisers.

- In the hospital setting, it is useful if the person can keep his or her inhalers by the bed, but they must be asked to let the nurse know how often they have been used, if it is necessary to monitor dosage. (See Nursing consideration, below.)
- Examine package inserts for precise instructions, as there may be variations between products.
- Pharmacists are often the best-qualified people to give advice and instruction in the use of these devices.

Nursing consideration   It is fairly easy for a person to overdose themselves with an inhaler. For example, at home they may have been taking four or five puffs to gain relief, and then they are instructed in the proper technique; if they still take four puffs, they may well be doubling the received dosage. There is also the question of psychological dependence, when the person uses their inhaler indiscriminately, even at the thought of becoming breathless, or on feeling a draught. Some readers may well have nursed people with salbutamol overdosage, which has come about because of this phenomenon.

Tuberculosis

Tuberculosis is the infectious disease of the lungs caused by the tubercle bacillus, *Mycobacterium tuberculosis*. The incidence of this condition has fallen steadily in Britain throughout the last century, levelling off at about 9000 new cases a year since 1970. A substantial number of these occur in older people, and the comparatively high death rate has been attributed to under-reporting of symptoms by this age-group.[5]

The usual symptoms are cough, weight loss, weakness and haemoptysis, with occasional night sweats; surprisingly, breathlessness may not be a problem until the condition is advanced.

Skin testing for tuberculosis (Heaf or Mantoux tests) can be misleading in the elderly, false negatives and positives both being possible; for a discussion of this phenomenon, the reader is referred to Freeman.[5] The most reliable test is sputum culture for AFB (acid-fast bacilli).

Examples of potential nursing diagnoses

Diagnostic statements include those listed in the sections on pneumonia and emphysema, above. 'Social isolation' should be considered as a nursing diagnosis if barrier nursing is required.

Potential nursing interventions

Interventions include those listed in the previous sections, but may also include:

1 Maintenance of nutritional status with high protein, high carbohydrate diet.
2 Implementation of isolation measures, if indicated; if the condition is contagious, it may be necessary to teach the patient about covering the mouth whilst coughing, and the correct disposal of tissues.
3 Allaying possible fear of, and stigma attached to, the affected person by other patients/residents, family, and possibly even staff, by taking appropriate educative measures.

CHAPTER FOUR

Cardiovascular problems

Cardiovascular vascular diseases account for the greatest number of deaths among older people in the United Kingdom. Angina pectoris, myocardial infarction and hypertension are the commonest cardiovascular problems in this age group; others are peripheral vascular disease, atherosclerosis, and anaemia. Signs of health problems in this area are cardiac enlargement, abnormal cardiac sounds, fine moist rales and distended neck veins. Symptoms include dyspnoea on exertion, orthopnoea, tachycardia, anorexia, and nausea/vomiting. The development of signs and symptoms may be very insidious, and are often not even noticed (or heeded) by older people and carers. A common complaint, which often serves as an indicator, is of having cold hands and feet.

Nursing interventions usually consist of reducing cardiac workload, monitoring the effectiveness of digitalis and diuretic medication, and reducing sodium and fluid retention through diet. The purpose of this chapter is to guide the nurse in developing nursing diagnoses and interventions with the common health problems related to cardiovascular disease.

Myocardial infarction

Heart attack, or myocardial infarction (MI), is the result of the occlusion of a coronary artery or its branches, and it may be asymptomatic in the older person. Tissue damage and death of heart muscle always occur, by definition. Acute chest pain is often absent; pain, if any, may be in the shoulder or jaw, and there may be a vague feeling of indigestion. Symptoms can progress rapidly to shock and cardiac arrest.

Examples of potential nursing diagnoses

1 Alteration in comfort due to pain.
2 Alteration in tissue perfusion due to erratic cardiac filling.
3 Fear of impending death.

Nursing priorities

1 Assess physical status and monitor vital signs.
2 Obtain emergency medical assistance.
3 Institute emergency life-saving measures if necessary.

Potential nursing interventions

1 Relief of pain, discomfort.

   • Place person in position of greatest comfort.
   • Loosen any constricting clothing.
   • Note location, quality, onset and duration of any pain.
   • Take a subjective measurement of pain: one way to do this is
     to ask the person to rate their pain on a scale of 1 to 10, with
     10 being the most severe.

2 Improve tissue perfusion.

   • Administer oxygen.
   • Monitor pulse and blood pressure continuously, if the equip-
     ment to do so is available; failing that, keep the intervals as
     short as is congruent with maintaining the patient's comfort.
     Auscultate heart sounds.
   • Observe for mottling of the skin, paleness, cyanosis, dia-
     phoresis, tightening of the shoulder girdle, and neck vein
     distension.

3 Relieve fear and anxiety.

   • Keep the environment as calm and quiet as possible.
   • Stay with the affected person at all times; use other people to
     summon assistance and 'fetch and carry'.
   • Remove all unnecessary persons from the area, but ensure
     that if the patient has, or is expecting, visitors, that someone
     has been detailed to look after them.

Nursing consideration Some elderly care units have 'positive resuscitation' policies, which state that CPR should *only* be initiated for patients who have been designated as being for active treatment in the event of cardiac or respiratory arrest. Others have no real policy at all, decisions being left to the nurse in charge at the time; and on occasion that person may not be able to explain satisfactorily why a particular decision was made, if questioned later. Nurses need to be very clear in their own minds about when resuscitation is indicated, and when it is not.[1]

Congestive cardiac failure (CCF)

Congestive cardiac failure (CCF) is the condition in which cardiac output is inadequate in relation to the body's needs. Mental confusion, insomnia, wandering about during the night, and peripheral and presacral oedema are possible signs.[2] A hacking cough, distended neck veins, and rapid weight gain may also be noted. An S_3 (third heart sound) may be heard in CCF.

Examples of potential nursing diagnoses

1 Decreased cardiac output due to increased cardiac workload.
2 Alteration in comfort due to chest pain, dyspnoea.
3 Alteration in fluid volume, more than body requirements, due to ineffective cardiac pumping.
4 Potential for fluid volume deficit due to use of diuretics.
5 Potential for impairment of skin integrity due to immobility and stasis.

Potential nursing interventions

1 Decrease the workload of the heart to improve cardiovascular status.

   • Monitor vital signs; take apical pulse rate.
   • Assess heart and lung sounds; be aware of possible S_3 being heard.
   • Maintain bedrest during acute phase; record vital signs after activity.

58

- When changing an occupied bed, change linen from the head of the bed down, instead of from side to side, to decrease cardiac workload for the patient.
- Plan and space activities to avoid unnecessary fatigue.
- Give assistance with eating, if necessary.

2 Relieve chest pain, discomfort.

- Place the person in a semi- or high-sitting/lying position.
- Provide overbed table for the person to adopt the orthopnoeic position, if necessary.

3 and 4 Maintain adequate/proper fluid balance.

- Record and monitor intake and output.
- Weigh daily, at the same time, and with the same scales.
- Observe for oedema; measure and record abdominal or peripheral girth daily.
- If fluids are restricted, give frequent mouth care; offer ice cubes, sugar-free boiled sweets or gum (unless contraindicated). Ice must be recorded on the fluid chart.
- Observe for signs of hypokalaemia if diuretics are being used (especially frusemide, but not when given with amiloride as co-amilofruse). Signs and symptoms include malaise, muscle weakness, faint heart sounds, and 'gassy' abdominal distension.[3]

5 Maintain skin integrity.

- If indicated, use sheepskins and/or any other pressure-relieving device.
- Change the position of the bedfast person at intervals of two hours or less, if he is unable to do so for himself.
- Check all pressure areas according to need, as defined by pressure sore risk calculation.

Hypertension

Age-related changes in blood pressure were discussed in the preceding section. Older persons who have a high blood pressure frequently awaken with a dull headache, have impaired memory, and may have epistaxis.

Examples of potential nursing diagnoses

1 Alteration in tissue perfusion due to increased cardiac workload.
2 Alteration in comfort, headache.
3 Potential for injury, falls, associated with weakness and/or dizziness.

Potential nursing interventions

1 Decrease the myocardial workload.

- Monitor the blood pressure in both arms with the person sitting, lying and standing.
- Encourage rest periods throughout the day and following activity.
- Teach relaxation techniques. There are many texts available which give advice on this subject.

2 Relieve discomfort, headache.

- Eliminate or decrease agents that may cause vasoconstriction, such as caffeine and nicotine. Contrary to the belief held by some practitioners, ice water can safely be given without danger of vasoconstriction.[4]
- Limit physical activity to a level congruent with maintaining independence.

3 Prevent injury, falls.

- Teach the person to rise slowly from the bed or chair, and to pause for a few moments before starting to walk.
- Instruct the person to sit or lie down and to summon help, if dizziness occurs.
- Keep the bed in a low position.

Nursing considerations

1 Blood pressure needs to be closely monitored if hypertensive medications have been prescribed, particularly after the first few doses, since the person may sustain a lowering of blood pressure to a point where hypotension becomes the problem.
2 To control or slow epistaxis, bend the head slightly forward, apply an ice pack to the back of the neck, and exert gentle pressure on the lower part of the nose by pinching the nostrils together for at least ten minutes.

60

Angina pectoris

Angina pectoris (more commonly referred to as 'angina', although this word just means 'pain'), is a chest pain due to decreased oxygenation of the myocardium. It is often less severe in older adults than younger ones, often manifesting itself as a vague feeling of indigestion.

Examples of potential nursing diagnoses

1 Alteration in comfort due to chest pain.
2 Potential for injury, falls, due to weakness.
3 Potential for impairment of skin integrity due to application of nitrate 'patches' or ointments.

Potential nursing interventions

1 Relieve chest pain.

   ● Administer medication as ordered.
   ● Decrease physical activity.
   ● Provide small, frequent meals to decrease cardiac workload.

2 Prevent potential injury, falls.

   ● Instruct the person to sit or lie down at first perception of pain, chest tightness or discomfort.
   ● Encourage the person to rest after meals and activity.
   ● If a nitrate such as glyceryl trinitrate (GTN) is prescribed for relief of symptoms, the person should recline for a few minutes after use, to prevent dizziness.

3 Maintain skin integrity.

   ● Rotate and record ointment or patch application sites; one useful method with patches is to put an arrow on them, indicating where the next day's patch should be placed.
   ● Carefully cleanse the area after a patch is removed. If the skin appears to be extremely sensitive, it is worth considering a change of the route of administration.
   ● Record and report reddened, irritated areas to the physician.

1   Caution must be used to avoid self-absorption of nitrates (for example GTN, 2 per cent ointment) when applying them to the skin.

2   Patches are ineffective if applied over the sternum, spine (or any bony prominence) and scar tissue.

Lenegre's disease

Lenegre's disease is described as a process in which microscopic lesions develop in both bundle branches of the cardiac conduction system. The coronary arteries and myocardium are not involved. Symptoms include fainting, loss of consciousness and seizures.[5]

Examples of potential nursing diagnoses

1   Alteration in cardiac output, decreased heart rate.
2   Potential for injuries, falls.

Potential nursing interventions

1   Decrease cardiac workload.

- Monitor vital signs, especially after activity.
- Investigate medication and dietary intake, to identify or exclude predisposing factors.

2   Prevent injuries, falls.

- Teach the person to recline or sit down upon onset of symptoms.
- Implement seizure precautions, if indicated.

Nursing considerations

1   Ensure that there is an airway of the correct size at the patient's bedside.

2   Have suction equipment 'ready to go'.

3   If siderails (cot sides) are to be used, ensure that they have been fitted with cushioning pads.

4   All staff need to be aware that the person may have seizures, in order to act appropriately and efficiently should an attack occur.

5   Never attempt to force the person's jaws open or restrain his limbs, during a seizure.

6   Remove the person's dentures only if they are occluding the airway.

7   If it is necessary to insert an airway (Brooke's, Guedel, etc.), ease it between the teeth when the jaws start to relax.

8   Record the time and duration of the seizure, whether consciousness was lost, and whether any body parts were involved.

Other considerations

Digitalis preparations (for example digoxin, digitoxin, lanatoside C) are frequently prescribed for older people with heart problems; but due to normal changes in the ageing body, as well as disease-induced changes, they can soon build up to toxic levels. Symptoms of toxicity include persistent nausea, weakness, vertigo, visual disturbances such as greenish-yellow vision, and hallucinations and nightmares.

The pulse must always be monitored before these drugs are given. If the pulse is below 60 beats per minute, check the apical rate; if this is also below 60, the drug should be withheld, the reason documented, and medical staff informed. Whenever possible, a person taking digitalis preparations should be instructed to monitor his or her own pulse rate.

Anaemias

Older people often become anaemic for a variety of reasons. It may be because of chronic insidious blood loss, due to haemorrhoids or gastrointestinal bleeding associated with long-term use of non-steroidal anti-inflammatory drugs; or it could be related to poor nutrition. Ill-fitting dentures, dental or periodontal problems can stop the person from eating properly. Additionally, older people with impaired mobility and/or vision may have extreme difficulty with shopping and cooking; and limited finances may reduce the amount of 'healthy foods' that the person can buy. Older people who live alone may fail to eat properly because of loneliness or depression, or simply because they do not like eating alone.[6] People with anaemia complain of weakness, anorexia, hypersensitivity to cold, and other vague complaints that others may attribute to 'old age'. As the anaemia advances, mental confusion may occur. A

63

thorough medical examination, as well as a dietary history, should always be made.

Iron deficiency anaemia

Iron deficiency is the most common cause of anaemia in older people. The condition is easily corrected with iron supplements, but these are often gastric irritants. Absorption is better on an empty stomach, but because of the problem of irritation, some authorities recommend giving the first few doses with food.

Example of potential nursing diagnosis

1   Alteration in nutrition, less than body requirements, related to inadequate dietary intake of iron.

Potential nursing intervention

1   Maintain adequate nutrition and iron intake

- Assess the condition of the mouth, teeth and any dentures (if any)
- Encourage dietary intake of foods high in iron, such as liver, beans, and dark green vegetables such as broccoli.
- Initially administer oral iron preparation with food; if no side-effects occur, administer on an empty stomach for better absorption (although the British National Formulary says that this is not essential).[7]

Pernicious anaemia

This form of anaemia is also common amongst older people, and is due to the lack of a specific factor in the gastric secretions (the 'intrinsic factor') necessary for the absorption of vitamin B_{12} (the 'extrinsic factor'). People with pernicious anaemia usually complain of a sore tongue (which appears reddened and ridged), weakness, and numbing and tingling of the extremities. They may not be able to feel vibration, and may have loss of the Achilles tendon reflex. The treatment simply consists of monthly or tri-monthly injections of Vitamin B_{12}.

Examples of potential nursing diagnoses

1 Alteration in nutrition, less than body requirements, due to glossitis.
2 Sensory perceptual alteration, coldness related to alteration in temperature.
3 Potential for injury, falls, bruises, associated with increased risk of falling due to weakness.

Potential nursing interventions

1 Maintain adequate nutrition, body weight.

 • Provide oral hygiene before and after meals with a very soft brush or cotton ball.
 • Avoid foods that are hot or highly seasoned.

2 Keep the person warm, avoid chilling. (See also interventions listed in Chapter 10, 'Hypothyroidism'.)

3 Prevent injuries.

 • Observe for changes in gait.
 • Assist with ambulation if necessary.
 • Teach the person to rise and move unhurriedly.

CHAPTER FIVE

Urinary problems and problems of the reproductive organs

One of the most distressing health problems that the older person can face is incontinence. The healthy older adult tends to pass urine more frequently, with an increased degree of urgency; but other potential problems include urinary tract infections (UTIs), neurogenic disorders and amongst males, prostatic hypertrophy. Control of urinary elimination is vital to the older person, not just for social and hygienic reasons, but also for maintenance of self-esteem.

The purpose of this chapter is to provide information to guide the nurse in formulating and developing nursing diagnoses, and selecting nursing interventions, for the patient or client with problems of the genitourinary system.

Urinary problems

Incontinence

Incontinence, the involuntary voiding of the bladder, is the chief urinary problem of older people. This condition may be due to multiple causes, including weakness of the muscles, inability of the kidneys to concentrate urine, neurological problems, certain medications, and mechanical causes such as calculi and prostatic enlargement,[1] but perhaps the commonest cause is faecal impaction. Additional causes can include dehydration, poor vision, which affects locating the toilet, and alteration in mobility.

Examples of potential nursing diagnoses

1. Alteration in urinary elimination, incontinence.
2. Self-care deficit related to inability to use toilet independently.

3. Potential for infection due to wetness, perineal irritation.
4. Disturbance in self-concept related to incontinence.
5. Knowledge deficit, urinary control measures.

Potential nursing interventions

1 Assess the cause of incontinence.

- Observe and record episodes of incontinence to determine whether or not there is a pattern. There are several charts available for this sort of monitoring, most of which are produced by companies who manufacture continence aids, but it is fairly easy to produce one's own. Basically, they record the times at which a person was dry or otherwise, and the frequency of toileting. Such charts must be scrupulously maintained for at least a week, if a reliable picture is to be obtained, as there are many singular occurrences that may distort the picture over a shorter period.
- Check for faecal impaction by digital (p.r.) examination. Gently percuss the abdomen for signs of bladder distension.
- Inspect external genitalia for redness, irritation and discharge. The perineal area should be washed gently with mild soap and water, then rinsed and thoroughly dried. A moisturising cream may be of help.
- Collect a urine sample. Examine the specimen for colour, cloudiness, purulence and odour, then perform a 'dipstick' test. Send a midstream specimen of urine (MSU, MSSU) for microscopy, culture and sensitivity, if there are any abnormalities.
- Review medications for potential side effects related to incontinence; some hypnotics, antidepressants, anxiolytics and sedatives are commonly found to be at the root of incontinence.
- Assess the environment. Determine if the toilet seat is too low or too high: if it is the too low, use a 'high-rise' toilet seat; if too high, provide a commode. Assess the lighting in the bathroom; it should be well-lit, but glare-free. If the toilet is a long way from the patient's or resident's bed area, and they cannot be moved, it may be necessary to provide a commode. Ensure privacy.
- Assess hydration; fluid intake should not fall below 1500–2000 ml/day, unless there are medical reasons for fluid restriction.

Provide fluids that acidify the urine, such as cranberry and citrus fruit juices, if liked; however, it should be remembered that some conditions, such as cystitis, respond to *alkalinisation* of the urine. Decrease the intake of caffeine, as this may promote diuresis and urgency.

2   Assist with toileting to maintain dryness.

- Encourage the use of the toilet or bedside commode, unless this is impossible.
- Design a realistic toileting schedule, involving the patient/ client in its planning. Assist with using the toilet before and after meals, planned activities, and bedtime.
- Facilitate voiding by running water when urination is desired. (The person may have some method of their own, such as blowing into a glass of water with a straw, whistling or placing their bare feet on a cold surface.)
- After assessing the continence chart, toilet the person before the usual times of episodes.
- Assess and record 'cues' for the need to void, if a communication deficit exists; these may include restlessness, agitation, or touching the lower abdominal/perineal area.

3   Provide personal hygiene to prevent infection.

- Cleanse area as described in item 1, above.
- Use soft, absorbent bathroom or facial tissue after voiding. Evaluate the effectiveness of the person's ability to maintain perineal hygiene.

4   Maintain the person's positive self-image.

- Praise all efforts to maintain continence.
- Never reprimand if incontinence occurs.
- Involve the person fully in all stages of planning, implementing and evaluating their continence programme.

5   Teach measures to promote urine control.

- Determine the length of time necessary to reach the bathroom or commode. Teach the person to allow adequate time to reach the toilet.

- Teach methods, such as pelvic floor exercises, which can increase muscle strength. Instruct the person to practice tightening the anal sphincter, as if attempting to hold back stool; and if possible, suggest the method of starting and stopping the stream of urine in flow, to increase meatal control.

Bladder infections (UTIs)

Bladder infections are the most common cause of fever in older people. Common symptoms include burning, urgency and abdominal pain; as the infection progresses, there may be retention of urine, haematuria and incontinence. Acute infections may be medically managed with antibiotics and/or antiseptics, but there is a growing body of opinion which states that there is no point in using such measures in chronic UTI.[2]

Examples of potential nursing diagnoses

1. Alteration in urinary elimination related to frequency, urgency.
2. Alteration in comfort due to abdominal pain, burning

Potential nursing interventions

1. Restore the normal voiding patterns.

   - Increase fluid intake unless contraindicated by other health problems.
   - Provide beverages that acidify the urine, if liked (but see item 1, above).
   - Provide a commode if the person has mobility problems, or if the bathroom is too distant.
   - Use disposable incontinence products if necessary, to avoid embarrassment and wetness.

2. Relieve pain related to infection.

   - Apply moist compresses to the perineal area.
   - Carefully cleanse perineum after voiding and bowel movements.
   - If the person is able to do so, he or she may benefit form soaking in a bath filled with warm water to the level of the umbilicus.

- Record the person's temperature at the same time each day, and be alert for rises in temperature, however slight; these may indicate fever in the older person.

Benign prostatic hypertrophy

Benign prostatic hypertrophy, or enlargement of the prostate gland, is present to some degree in the majority of older men. Initially, symptoms of frequency, nocturia, decreased urinary force, dribbling and inability to initiate voiding occur; as the condition progresses, there is urinary retention, pains in the flank and/or lower abdomen, and haematuria. If unrecognised and uncorrected, kidney damage due to hydronephrosis may occur.

Surgical intervention is usually very successful, since the advent of the transurethral resection of prostate (TURP) coupled with the availability of epidural anaesthesia; however, a sizable number of doctors practising in Britain will try to manage the condition with drugs that assist with the emptying of the bladder (for example, emepronium bromide), or catheterisation.

Examples of potential nursing diagnoses

1 Alteration in urinary elimination related to inability to empty the bladder.
2 Sleep pattern disturbance due to nocturia.
3 Alteration in comfort, pain, due to bladder distension.

Potential nursing interventions

1 Relieve urinary retention.

- Record intake and output.
- Gently palpate and percuss suprapubic area to identify bladder distension.
- Ensure a fluid intake of 1500–2000 ml/day, if other medical considerations permit.
- Catheterise only if absolutely necessary.
- Assist or instruct the person to stand when voiding.

2 Promote sleep/rest.

- Some individuals *may* benefit from restricting fluids in the hour or so before bedtime, but each person must be carefully assessed before such a regime is suggested.

- Check for bladder emptying and/or distension at bedtime.
- Use disposable incontinence products during the night if leakage is a problem.

3 Relieve pain due to bladder distension (see measures suggested under 'Bladder infections' on page 69).

Indwelling catheters

It is never desirable for older people to have permanent indwelling catheters; infections and inflammation seem to occur without fail, although this is probably attributable to poor management.[3] However, there are times when the use of a catheter is essential. Meticulous perineal and meatal care must be performed for the older person, especially after bowel movements. Indwelling catheters may be lightly taped, allowing some slack, to the inside of the thigh, to facilitate drainage and prevent pulling on the catheter; there are also many products on the market for the discreet attachment of catheter drainage bags to clothing or the leg, where they are not open to view.

When caring for uncircumcised males, the caregiver must make certain that the foreskin is replaced over the glans penis; failure to do so can lead to painful swelling of the glans ('paraphimosis'), which may, in turn, lead to tissue necrosis.

Examples of potential nursing diagnoses

1 Potential for infection due to indwelling catheter.
2 Alteration in urinary elimination related to catheterisation.

Potential nursing interventions

1 Prevent urinary tract infection.

- Provide perineal care.
- Maintain a closed drainage system, obtaining samples only through the aspiration ports; never use spigots.
- Do not routinely irrigate catheters; this procedure should only be done when absolutely necessary (for example to clear a blockage).
- Do not routinely change catheters; refer to the manufacturers' recommendations as to the length of time their make can be left in situ. Otherwise, change only when patency is impaired.

71

2 Attempt to restore normal voiding pattern by removing the catheter at the first safe opportunity.

Nursing considerations There is a great deal of disagreement amongst practitioners regarding the necessity for some form of bladder retraining *before* catheter removal; but whatever method is used, the procedure should be carefully planned, and the patient involved in that planning.

Problems of the reproductive organs

Many older women believe that gynaecological examinations are not necessary after the childbearing age, menopause or hysterectomy. Although the incidence of cervical cancer declines with age, examinations must be continued to detect other types of malignancies as well as benign conditions of the reproductive system.

Vaginitis (atrophic vaginitis, leucorrhoea)

Vaginitis is a common problem of older women. Symptoms include vaginal discharge, soreness and itching. Confused or noncommunicative persons may be restless and scratch the genital area.

Examples of potential nursing diagnoses

1 Alteration in comfort; pain and itching.
2 Potential for impairment of skin and mucous membrane integrity due to irritation.
3 Knowledge deficit, need for gynaecological examinations.

Potential nursing interventions

1 Relieve pain and itching.

- Maintain perineal hygiene. Wash the area with mild soap and water, rinse well and dry thoroughly. Apply prescribed topical preparations, or use a moisturising cream.
- Apply moist compresses to the affected area.
- If vaginal suppositories or creams are prescribed, instil medication while the person is lying in bed, to achieve the best effect. The side-lying position may be used; this is usually more dignified than the 'straddle'.

72

2 Maintain integrity of perineal tissues.

- Institute hygienic measures outlined above.
- Provide warm baths, avoiding excessively high temperatures which may damage fragile tissue.
- If douching is ordered, select the size carefully, to avoid tissue injury. Monitor the solution temperature; pre-packed solutions may need warming.

3 Health teaching, need for gynaecological examination.

- Explain the need for the procedure or examination.
- Explain the procedure itself.

Prolapse

Prolapse of the uterus or other pelvic part may occur among older women as a result of the stretching and tearing of muscles during childbirth, or because of muscle weakness associated with ageing. Signs and symptoms may include visible protrusion of parts, low back pain, and pelvic 'pulling'.

Examples of potential nursing diagnoses and interventions

Nursing diagnoses and interventions include those cited in the previous section. Additional interventions might include:

1 Observe and record the time, frequency and appearance of the prolapsed part.
2 Protect the prolapsed part with sterile lubricated gauze and padding.
3 If possible, have the person lie down and assume the knee–chest position to reduce the prolapse.
4 A referral to a gynaecologist may be of use.

CHAPTER SIX

Gastrointestinal problems

Common health problems of the gastrointestinal system consists of difficulties with ingestion, digestion and elimination – processes that may interfere with adequate nutrition. The purpose of this chapter is to provide the nurse with information about identifying potential or actual nursing diagnoses and interventions for older people suffering from the more common health problems related to the gastrointestinal system.

Xerostomia

The condition of the mouth and teeth is a primary consideration in sound nutrition. Periodontal disease can predispose the older person to systemic infection. Xerostomia, or dryness of the oral mucosa, may result from decreased production of saliva and/or medications with anticholinergic (antimuscarinic) effects, something commonly associated with the tricyclic antidepressants. Good oral hygiene is especially important for older people, who have losses in the number of taste buds.

Example of potential nursing diagnosis

1. Potential for impairment of oral mucosa.

Potential nursing intervention

1. Maintain integrity of the teeth and oral mucosa:

   - Brush the teeth and tongue with a soft toothbrush or foam brush after each meal. Gentle flossing may also be done.

Nursing consideration Mouth care is perhaps one of the most contentious areas in British nursing practice today. For an excellent discussion, see Ford and Walsh on the subject.[1]

Hiatal hernia

Hiatal (hiatus) hernia is the protrusion of the proximal portion of the stomach into the thoracic cavity, through the diaphragm. In the United States, it has been suggested that 67 per cent of people over the age of 60 may have a hiatus hernia,[2] whilst in the United Kingdom, one large survey confirmed that it it is a condition whose incidence increases with age, 82 per cent of sufferers being over 50.[3]

Signs and symptoms include heartburn, belching, and vomiting after meals, especially when reclining or bending forward. The condition is aggravated by increased intra-abdominal pressure.

Examples of potential nursing diagnoses

1. Alteration in comfort due to pain.
2. Alteration in nutrition, less than body requirements, due to inability or reluctance to eat and retain food.

Potential nursing interventions

1 Relieve discomfort.

- Position the patient after meals in as upright a position as he can tolerate.
- Do not feed the person in bed, unless sitting up is impossible or contraindicated.
- Avoid increasing intra-abdominal pressure by encouraging the person to wear loose-fitting clothes, avoiding corsets if possible. Prevent constipation.

2 Maintain weight and adequate nutrition:

- Provide food in portions 'little and often', instead of as three meals a day. (See Nursing consideration, below.)
- Supplement diet with high-protein additions, if necessary.
- Instruct the person to eat slowly, and to maintain an upright position for 30 minutes after each meal.[4]

Nursing consideration 'Little and often' is a very imprecise term; but if intake is translated into calories/day, that imprecision can be avoided.

Diverticulitis

Diverticuli, or multiple pouches of the mucosa of the colon, are very common among older people. For the great majority, they cause no problems; their presence is called diverticulosis, and this is not a health problem unless the pouches become full of bowel contents which harden and set off an inflammatory reaction called diverticulitis. There is usually pain in the left lower abdominal quadrant, and often there is a history of constipation in the preceding days. Hospitalisation may be necessary during an acute attack.

Examples of potential nursing diagnoses

1 Alteration in comfort, pain.
2 Alteration in bowel elimination, constipation.
3 Alteration in fluid balance, less than body requirements, due to nausea.
4 Alteration in nutrition, less than body requirements, due to loss of appetite, nausea.

Potential nursing interventions

1 Relieve abdominal pain.

● Assess abdomen for presence, absence or hyperactivity of bowel sounds, pain, tenderness or distension; record findings.
● Apply ice pack to the abdomen, if pain is severe, until the go-ahead is given for analgesia.

2 Prevent constipation.

● Encourage high-residue diet, if obstruction has been ruled out, and fluids to a minimum of 1500–2000 ml/day, if other medical considerations permit.
● Having established the person's normal bowel habit, ensure that stool is being passed regularly; if not, consider the use of aperients and/or suppositories.
● Avoid the use of phosphate or other large-volume enemas, which may cause bowel irritation.

3 Maintain adequate hydration.

● Assess mucous membranes for moisture; gently palpate eye-balls for 'mushiness' (a sign of dehydration); assess skin turgor.

- Record input and output if urine output falls below 30 ml/hr.

4   Maintain weight, adequate nutrition.

- Provide a high-fibre diet (but see item 2, above) and dietary supplements, guided by advice from the dietitian.
- Weigh the person every 2 to 4 weeks, ensuring that the same scales are used each time.

Gallbladder disease

The commonest reason for abdominal surgery in the elderly, it has been suggested, is biliary tract disease,[5] and it has also been identified, unsurprisingly, as the most common cause of severe abdominal pain.[6] Fever is present, and pain is in the upper right abdominal quadrant. Surgery, if indicated, is often postponed until the person's condition is improved. Persons with gallbladder disease often report intolerance of certain foods: pork and other fatty foods are frequently cited.

Examples of potential nursing diagnoses

Diagnostic statements include those cited under 'hiatal hernia' and 'diverticulitis' on pages 75 and 76. Additional diagnostic statements may include:

1   Alteration in nutrition, less than body requirements,due to food intolerance.
2   Potential for impairment of skin integrity due to accumulation of bile salts in the blood, which causes pruritus.

Potential nursing interventions

1   Maintain adequate nutrition.

- Assess for food intolerances.
- Substitute other foods that do not cause distress, to provide adequate nutrition.

2   Maintain skin integrity.
- Observe sclera for yellowing.
- Shake urine and look for frothing (if bile is present, the urine will foam).
- Do not use soap on the skin, but keep it lubricated with a suitable unperfumed moisturiser (such as aqueous cream).

Haemorrhoids

Haemorrhoids (ano-rectal varicose veins), while usually asymptomatic, may cause health problems for older people. The person may complain of intense itching and/or pain in the anal area. Streaks of bright red blood may appear in the stool, on toilet paper, or on undergarments. Haemorrhoids are aggravated by constipation, sitting for long periods, and frequent p.r. examination. Constipation is often the result of the person postponing defecation, in an attempt to avoid pain.

Examples of potential nursing diagnoses

1 Alteration in comfort, pain.
2 Alteration in bowel elimination, constipation.

Potential nursing interventions

1 Relieve anal/rectal pain.

- Observe and record episodes of blood in the stool.
- Provide a pressure relieving pad, such as an oil-filled or a Roho cushion, for the person to sit on.
- Wash and dry anal area carefully with a soft cloth or tissue.
- Use ice packs initially on the anal area, to reduce oedema and assist retraction of the haemorrhoids; after 15–20 minutes, use warm compresses or immersion to soothe and promote circulation.
- Do not perform rectal examinations unless it is absolutely essential.

2 Prevent constipation. (See the next section of this chapter.)

Nursing consideration Haemorrhoids are often treated as a subject for humour in Britain – except by those who have them, or have nursed people with problems that have arisen because of them. The condition is an extremely painful one, and can lead to significant blood loss; this should be borne in mind when dealing with patients who are apologetic and embarrassed about needing treatment, or their families, who may say on learning the diagnosis, 'Is that all it was?'

Constipation/faecal impaction

Constipation and faecal impaction are common problems amongst older people: inactivity, immobility, less dietary bulk, reduced fluid intake, and laxative abuse are all aggravating factors. The best measures are preventative ones.

Examples of potential nursing diagnoses

1 Alteration in bowel elimination, constipation/faecal impaction.
2 Knowledge deficit related to diet, resulting in constipation.

Potential nursing interventions

1 Prevent constipation.

- Record bowel elimination to determine a cycle or pattern.
- Maintain adequate fluid intake.
- Provide high fibre diet; if indicated, consider obtaining a prescription for stool softeners and/or bulking agents (for example lactulose, ispaghula husk).
- Determine what practices the person uses to initiate a bowel movement, and implement if possible.
- If a bowel movement has not occurred after the desired interval established in the first intervention in this list, consider the use of a suppository or enema (see item 2, below).

2 Relieve faecal impaction.

- Assess for impaction by gently performing a digital examination of the rectum. Explain the procedure carefully. Position the person on their left side, and gently insert a well-lubricated, gloved finger through the anus, and carefully palpate for faeces. A topical anaesthetic ointment may be helpful, but it must be prescribed.
- If the stool is soft, it is not impacted, and should respond to aperients or suppositories, should natural methods fail. If it is hard, a stool-softening enema such as sodium docusate, as a micro-enema, or arachis oil, as a retention enema given at night, will assist with evacuation.
- If the above methods fail, it may be necessary to remove the impacted faeces manually. Two gloved and lubricated fingers

can be inserted to break hard stool into smaller pieces that can be evacuated or removed. It is essential to remember that this is a potentially lethal procedure, which must *never* be carried out by an unskilled, unsupervised person. In some areas, it may be necessary to obtain medical permission for this procedure.

- After manual removal of stool, a small enema may be given to assist with evacuation of the remaining faeces; micro-enemas of 5ml are now widely available.

Nursing considerations Large-volume enemas should not be given to the older person at all, if possible, as shock may result from the sudden distension of the large bowel.[7] When trying to determine the causes of constipation, a good question to ask is: Was lack of privacy, or potential embarrassment, a factor? Bed curtains do not provide a very effective smell or sound barrier.

CHAPTER SEVEN

Musculoskeletal problems

Osteoporosis and osteoarthritis are common health problems that effect changes in balance, posture and mobility in older adults. Some of the most common health problems of older people are related to changes that occur in muscles, bones and joints. The older person is at high risk for falls and fractures. There is often a fine line that distinguishes pathology from the normal changes that come with ageing. The purpose of this chapter is to provide information about musculoskeletal problems of the older person and to assist the nurse in developing nursing diagnoses with possible nursing interventions for the client with these problems.

Osteoporosis

Osteoporosis is the most common bone disease affecting older people; it is characterised by demineralisation of bone, resulting in decreased bone mass and density.[1] Immobilisation accelerates this condition. Older people often believe that pain, which frequently occurs in the vertebrae and lower limbs, is due to 'rheumatism'. The exact cause of osteoporosis is not known, but its development is related to the dietary intake of calcium, protein and phosphate, metabolism of vitamin D, and deficits of oestrogen. Compression fractures of the vertebrae are a common complication of osteoporosis.

Examples of potential nursing diagnoses

1 Impaired physical mobility due to stiffness.
2 Alteration in comfort, pain.
3 Potential for physical injury, fracture.
4 Knowledge deficit related to dietary intake of calcium, protein, and phosphate.

Potential nursing interventions

1 Improve mobility by increasing muscle strength.

- Obtain physiotherapy assessment.
- Encourage sedentary exercises, such as arm extensions, arm curls, stationary rocking, and other range of motion (ROM) exercises.
- Avoid prolonged immobility.

2 Relieve pain.

- Take a careful history to determine precipitating factors such as certain activities, temperature variations and so on which may result in pain.
- Try to give prescribed medication *before* the expected onset of pain.

3 Prevent falls, fractures.

- Encourage the proper use of frames, sticks, or other mobility aids.
- Instruct the person to rise slowly from the bed or chair.
- Check footwear; well-fitting, low-heeled shoes should be worn, and slippers avoided, if possible.
- Use great care and gentleness when moving or exercising the person with osteoporosis.

4 Instruct the person about foods that are high in calcium, protein and phosphate.

- Refer to dietitian.
- Encourage the selection of foods with the necessary nutrients.

Nursing consideration Height loss accompanies the development of osteoporosis, due to the gradual vertebral collapse. One way of assessing the amount of spinal compression is to have the person raise their arms sideways, to shoulder level; the distance from the longest fingertip of one hand to the other is then measured. In non-diseased people, this measurement is the same as the person's height; but when there has been vertebral compression, it exceeds the height.[2]

Osteoarthritis

Osteoarthritis is the gradual thinning of joint cartilage. Symptoms include aching, stiffness and limited motion of joints; the knee is most frequently affected. Characteristic nodules or thickenings, known as Heberden's nodes, often appear at the distal joints of fingers. Whilst these nodes are disfiguring, they are not disabling. Their appearance helps differentiate osteoarthritis from rheumatoid arthritis.[3] Additionally, inflammation is often absent in osteoarthritis. Medical management of this condition usually involves a combination of medication, physiotherapy and exercise. Whilst it is always inadvisable to limit a person's independence, people with osteoarthritis should be cautioned not to overdo things, because severe pain can follow unusual activity.

Examples of potential nursing diagnoses

1 Alteration in comfort, pain.
2 Impaired physical mobility due to joint stiffness.
3 Decreased activity tolerance due to immobility and pain.

Potential nursing interventions

1 Relieve arthritic pain.

- Determine what method(s) the affected person uses to relieve pain and implement them, if possible.
- Obtain a detailed medication history, including home remedies, to determine what has the best analgesic effect for that person.
- If warmth relieves the pain, apply moist heat to the affected areas.
- Use wool or sheepskin protectors on the affected joints to provide warmth and protection.
- Evaluate the effectiveness of all the above measures.

2 Improve physical mobility affected by joint stiffness.

- Obtain a physiotherapy opinion.
- Maintain proper body alignment; instruct the person about proper body mechanics.
- Maintain and promote an exercise programme, including ROM and isometric exercises.

83

- Under the guidance of the physiotherapist, encourage the use of the appropriate walking aids to promote stability and safety.

3 Improve activity tolerance, conserve strength.

- Determine which activities (ADLs, social, therapeutic) are most difficult or painful for the person.
- Give prescribed analgesia prior to activity times.
- Plan the sequence of all activities through the day, to conserve body resources.

Rheumatoid arthritis

Rheumatoid arthritis involves inflammatory changes in the synovial membrane, resulting in destruction of joint cartilage and deformities. Symptoms are extremely painful and swollen joints (especially in the mornings) fever, fatigue and a general malaise. Medical treatment is directed at the relief of inflammation. The exercise/therapy/activity plan must be carefully designed by the multi-disciplinary team (nurse, physio- and occupational therapists, medical staff and of course, the patient). People with this condition can frequently benefit from the use of assistive devices, such as specially designed cutlery and kitchen tools, to promote and maintain their independence.

Examples of potential nursing diagnoses

Diagnostic statements include those listed in the section on osteoarthritis, above.

Potential nursing interventions

Nursing interventions include those cited in the section on osteoarthritis.

Nursing considerations During exacerbations of the disease, it is essential to rest the affected body part(s). Splinting is sometimes used to protect those parts from further injury and to prevent joint contractures; but this is very controversial, some practitioners believing that contractures may be worsened by increased spasticity due to joint immobilisation.

The nurse must also be aware of the various side effects of drugs used in this condition, and closely monitor the patient for signs and symptoms associated with untoward reactions. Many, if not all, non-steroidal anti-inflammatory drugs (NSAIDs) are gastric irritants, and there is a high risk of peptic ulceration. Some doctors routinely prescribe H_2-antagonists, such as ranitidine or cimetidine, with NSAIDs associated with the highest risks (which, unfortunately, tend to be the most effective ones); but there is really no substitute for the vigilance of a nurse in monitoring patients.

Hip fractures

It has been estimated in the United States that as many as 45 per cent of women over the age of 75 and over sustain hip fractures.[4] These fractures may be due to many causes, including transient ischaemic attack, rapid drop in blood pressure, osteoporosis, and many others. The caregiver should always be concerned with the cause of the fracture. Occasionally, older persons may sustain these fractures without any pain being felt, so the nurse must look out for gait disturbances. On the other hand, there may be intense pain, requiring large doses of opiates to bring it under control. Signs include shortening of the leg on the affected side, external rotation, and spasm of the quadriceps muscle.

Examples of potential nursing diagnoses

1 Alteration in comfort due to pain.
2 Impaired physical mobility due to interruption of bone integrity.
3 Potential for impairment of skin integrity.
4 Potential for joint contractures.

Potential nursing interventions

1 Relieve pain.

   ● Give analgesia as prescribed, and monitor its effectiveness.
   ● Apply ice to fracture site, with care not to damage the skin.
   ● Immobilise the affected hip with splints, sandbags, or whatever is to hand.

2 Care following surgery depends on the operation performed; ambulation is resumed as soon as possible.

3 Prevent pressure sore formation.

- Institute pressure area care regime.
- Use pressure-relieving mattress, if available.

4 Prevent joint contractures.

- Maintain functional alignment in bed.
- Implement and teach range of motion (ROM) exercises.

CHAPTER EIGHT

Neurological disorders

The complexity of anatomy and function of the nervous system results in confusion between the normal ageing process and pathological processes. The most common health problems of the neurological system are presented in this chapter. Cerebrovascular accident, Parkinson's disease and acute and chronic brain syndromes, including dementia of the Alzheimer type, are discussed, with special emphasis on rehabilitative measures.

Cerebrovascular accident

In Great Britain, about 70 000 deaths every year can be attributed to cerebrovascular accident (CVA), or stroke, making it the third leading cause of death after heart disease and cancer.[1]

A CVA occurs when there is disruption to the brain's blood supply; unlike most other organs, the brain cannot survive for very long without the oxygen carried in the blood, and any sections affected will rapidly 'die off', without hope of regeneration. The principal underlying cause of stroke is atherosclerotic changes in the cerebral blood vessels, but dehydration, diabetes mellitus, anaemia, hypertension and atrial fibrillation can all be predisposing factors.

Signs and symptoms of stroke include hemiplegia or hemiparesis, sensory disturbances, particularly visual, and aphasia. Some readers will be used to a distinction between 'dysphasia' – disturbance of speech and/or understanding – and 'aphasia', in which either or both abilities are completely lost; it is now becoming common practice to use one word, aphasia, to cover both senses.

There is a time factor in the diagnosis of a stroke: if symptoms disappear within twenty-three hours and fifty-nine minutes, then the episode is classed as a 'transient ischaemic attack' (TIA); but once twenty-four hours have passed, if any symptoms remain, then it is designated a CVA.[2] TIAs often serve as a warning that a CVA is imminent.

The severity of a stroke depends upon the area of brain and amount of tissue affected. Damage to the right side of the brain results in paralysis of the left side of the body. There may be memory deficits, impulsive behaviour, and/or spatial–perceptual deficits. Damage to the left side of the brain results in paralysis of the right side of the body and slow, disorganised behaviour. Aphasia often results when the damage is on the left side of the brain; it may be *receptive*, that is, the person cannot understand what he reads, hears, or sees; or *expressive*, in which he can understand, but is unable to form speech or write comprehensibly. If both forms co-exist, it is called conduction aphasia.[3] Visual problems, known as hemianopia, also frequently occur with stroke. A right-sided CVA – that is, one which affects the left-hand side of the body – may be accompanied by an inability to see the left side of the visual field; both eyes are affected, but the person is unaware of this deficit. The effect is reversed in a left-sided CVA.

It is not surprising that deep depression and withdrawal often accompany a stroke, considering the number of losses that the victim sustains; but the sooner rehabilitation efforts start, the likelihood of some improvement is increased. Nursing the stroke victim is one of the hardest parts of care of the elderly – but it is potentially the most rewarding.

Examples of potential nursing diagnoses

1 Alteration in cerebral tissue perfusion related to compromised blood flow.
2 Ineffective airway clearance due to diminished cough reflex.
3 Potential for fluid volume deficit due to inability to swallow.
4 Alteration in nutrition, less than body requirements, due to inability to eat and drink.
5 Alteration in bowel elimination, constipation, due to immobility and dietary changes.
6 Alteration in urinary elimination due to immobility, fluid balance changes.
7 Impaired physical mobility (specify deficit, for example related to right/left hemiplegia).
8 Potential for joint contractures due to immobility.
9 Impaired communication, spoken and/or written.

10 Potential for impairment of skin integrity due to immobility.
11 Sensory-perceptual deficit, impaired vision.
12 Body image disturbance due to loss of function and sensory neglect.
13 Self care deficit (specify).

Potential nursing interventions

1 Monitor neurological status to ascertain changes in homoeostasis.

- Monitor and document vital signs; monitor femoral, popliteal and pedal pulses.
- Monitor and document pupil size, pupillary response to stimuli, presence/absence of speech, orientation to person/place.
- Monitor and record intake and output.

2 Facilitate coughing effort and airway clearance.

- Assess patency of airway; auscultate chest for adventitious sounds.
- Maintain adequate humidity to prevent drying of secretions.
- Position person to maximise coughing effort, airway clearance.
- Use suction only if necessary.

3 Maintain adequate hydration.

- Assess mucous membranes for moisture; gently palpate eyeballs and test skin turgor for signs of dehydration.
- See item 1, above.
- Assess integrity of gag reflex by gently touching the uvula with a cotton bud. The open mouth can be stabilised by inserting the index finger on the middle of the tongue and applying mild pressure.
- If the gag reflex is intact, the ability to swallow can be tested by instilling a small amount of fluid into the back of the mouth and instructing the person to swallow.

4 Maintain adequate nutrition.

- Assess swallowing ability as in item 3, above.
- Seat the person upright if possible.

89

- Offer chewable rather than semisoft or puréed foods. Chewing seems to enhance the swallowing reflex for some people.
- Check for proper denture fit, if applicable. If the dentures are a poor fit, the person's chewing and swallowing efforts will be enhanced by their removal.
- Stimulate the swallowing reflex by having the person suck briefly on an ice cube prior to eating. Immediately after the sucking, lightly stroke around the mouth with another ice cube, three times; then three times from both earlobes to the corners of the mouth. Finally, apply the ice to the sternal notch for not more than three seconds. After the icing procedure, repeat the movements with a sable or vibrating brush each time swallowing is required.[4]
- Prepare and place the food within the person's field of vision.
- Place the food in the unaffected side of the mouth. Use a mirror in front of the face to teach correct placement of food.
- Ensure privacy when feeding efforts are begun; do not give the person meals in a communal dining area until the person has gained confidence in the ability to swallow.
- Use specially designed utensils, or encase the handles of spoons and forks in foam to facilitate gripping; the occupational therapist is the best person to advise on this.

5 Prevent constipation (See Chapter 5, 'Constipation' and 'Faecal impaction' sections.)

6 Prevent urinary incontinence and retention. (See Chapter 6, 'Incontinence' section.)

7 Maintain optimal physical mobility.

- Assess and document extent of paralysis immediately, and at regular intervals thereafter.
- Immediately begin passive ROM exercises of all extremities, twice daily.
- Splint and protect affected limbs (but see Nursing considerations for rheumatoid arthritis, in Chapter 6).
- Pronate the person twice daily, if they can tolerate this.
- Maintain functional alignment in bed.

8 Prevent joint contractures.

- See item 7, above.
- Prevent shoulder contractures by supporting the arms with pillows or bath blankets when the person is in bed. As activity progresses, the affected arm may be supported by a 'hemi-cuff', or Bobath sling, which supports the weight of the upper arm and reduces the likelihood of subluxation.
- Use hard cones rather than soft materials to prevent contractures of the hand, as soft objects tend to promote flexion.[5]
- Use sandbags to prevent hip rotation.
- Do not use footboards to prevent footdrop; the pressure exerted on the ball of the foot, as well as being a potential source of tissue damage, actually stimulates plantar flexion.[6] The best preventative method is pronation (see item 7, above), with the feet being allowed to extend over the end of the mattress.

9 Establish and maintain communication.

- Determine the native language of the person, as aphasia can sometimes lead to a reversion to the first language spoken.[7]
- Talk directly to the person, using short, specific phrases and maintaining eye contact.
- Encourage the person to sing familiar rhymes/ditties to aid in communication. Even if speech is impaired, the ability to sing may not be.[8]
- Use communication boards and other equipment, as recommended by the speech therapist.

10 Prevent skin breakdown (See interventions listed in Chapter 11.)

11 Modify the environment to compensate for visual losses.

- Assess the scope of impairment (hemianopia, diplopia) through visual assessment. This may be accomplished by asking the person to point to pictures on a printed page.
- The following interventions must be carefully discussed by the multidisciplinary team before implementation, as they are mutually exclusive.

    (i) If the person does *not* have neglect of the affected side (see 12, below), position the person so that other people

91

and activities are perceived in the intact field of vision, and instruct all staff and visitors to approach the person from the visually intact side.

(ii) If neglect is present, reverse the actions given in (i) above; additionally, ensure that the person turns their head frequently towards the affected side, to get used to 'scanning' his or her environment.[9]

12 Increase and facilitate the person's awareness of the affected side.

- Teach the person to use the unaffected limbs in moving the affected part; for example, hooking one leg under the other to change its position.
- Encourage exercises in which the limbs cross the body's midline, such as swinging the arms from side to side, or using the unaffected arm to change the position of the other.
- Teach the person to gauge space and distance by over-estimating the size of doorways, lengths of halls, distances between starting and finishing points and so on.
- Never refer to the affected side as the 'bad' side; from the first moment, the emphasis must be on the positive, stressing the eventual regaining of at least some use in that side, or part of it.

Parkinson's disease

Parkinson's disease is a disorder of body movement characterised by four major signs.

1 Bradykinesia, or slowing of movement
2 The loss of postural reflexes
3 A 'pill-rolling' tremor at rest
4 Muscle rigidity.

Muscle rigidity often causes the greatest physical impairment.[10]

Other signs of this condition are a mask-like facial expression, a festinating (hurrying) gait, speech difficulties, and problems related to the autonomic nervous system, including sweating, urinary retention, constipation, postural hypotension, and excessive salivation which, when coupled with swallowing difficulties, leads to drooling.

The underlying cause is dysfunction of the brain's basal ganglia; these collections of nerve cells and supporting tissues are the centres of motor coordination. A neurotransmitter called dopamine is manufactured by specialised pigmented cells that make up the substantia nigra, which is located in the basal ganglia. In Parkinson's disease, there are losses of these cells and a consequent depletion of the amount of available dopamine.

The principal treatment of the condition is to increase the levels of dopamine, by giving drugs such as levodopa (which is converted to dopamine in the body), and others which make the binding of available dopamine in receptor cells more efficient; yet more drugs can be given to control tremor. Different people respond very differently to similar regimes, and much medical treatment in the newly-diagnosed person is by trial and error.

Involuntary movements are an unfortunate side-effect of levodopa therapy in some people, but there may be improvement with relatively small adjustments to the total daily dosage.[11] Other side-effects are nausea, vomiting, anorexia, urinary retention, and orthostatic hypotension. Sexual arousal sometimes occurs.[12]

The long-term use of phenothiazines (for example chlorpromazine, thioridazine and promazine, all of which may be prescribed for older people) can produce symptoms which closely resemble Parkinson's disease, and which are referred to as 'parkinsonism'; this is usually reversible, simply by discontinuing the drug.

Examples of potential nursing diagnoses

1 Impaired physical mobility related to bradykinesia and muscle rigidity.
2 Impaired verbal communication due to weakness of the muscles associated with speech production.
3 Alteration in nutrition, less than body requirements, due to difficulty in swallowing.
4 Potential for infection, pneumonia, due to weakness of chest muscles.
5 Alteration in urinary elimination, incontinence.
6 Alteration in bowel elimination, constipation.
7 Potential for impairment of skin integrity due to immobility.
8 Disturbance in self-concept related to physical losses.

Potential nursing interventions

1 Maintain/improve mobility.

- Carefully assess afflicted person to determine levels of mobility; reassess at regular intervals.
- Teach the person to set the feet down heels first when walking, and to increase the length of the stride.
- Teach the person to swing arms when walking, to improve balance.
- Encourage practising 'marching' to music.
- If 'freezing' occurs when the person is walking, teach the technique of 'unfreezing' by raising the arms or trying to step backwards.
- Teach the person to rise from the chair by placing feet apart and back, then pushing against the chair arms.
- Encourage practising fine motor function by picking up coins or marbles.
- Perform, or teach the person to perform, ROM exercises twice daily.

2 Improve and/or maintain verbal communication.

- Refer to the speech therapist.
- Teach the person to take a breath before initiating speech, and to start speaking on the outward breath.
- Encourage the person to practice exercises such as singing, reading aloud or repeating certain sounds, as directed by the speech therapist.

3 Maintain adequate nutrition.

- Provide the person with meals or trays at first to compensate for slowness in eating, until he or she feels ready to dine communally.
- Use specially designed cutlery to facilitate grasp.
- See other interventions listed under 'CVA', above.

4 Prevent respiratory infection. (See interventions listed in Chapter 3.)

5 Prevent urinary retention, incontinence. (See interventions listed in Chapter 5.)

94

6 Prevent constipation. (See interventions listed in Chapter 6.)

7 Maintain skin integrity; prevent skin breakdown. (See interventions listed in Chapter 11.)

8 Increase self-esteem.

- Always allow the person to express their thoughts and feelings.
- If appropriate, make a referral to a professional with counselling skills (for example, a clinical psychologist or community psychiatric nurse).
- Inform the patient/client about the benefits of medication.
- Encourage discussions that reflect on past successes.
- Provide positive reinforcement about intact physical abilities.

Organic brain diseases

When an older person suddenly becomes confused or has a personality change, it should be treated as an emergency. Diagnostic tests should be undertaken to determine the cause; confusion is never a normal or expected part of ageing. Organic brain diseases are the most debilitating of all ailments associated with ageing, in terms of human loss. The term 'organic brain disease', while frequently listed in records as the definitive medical diagnosis, is actually a very imprecise one, and may preclude thorough nursing assessment and interventions; it is better to classify these health problems more specifically as acute or chronic brain syndromes of a particular type, whenever possible. 'Acute' and 'chronic' are terms defined by times of onset. (For further discussion, see Chapter 12.)

Acute brain syndrome

Acute brain syndrome has a rapid onset. Symptoms include misidentification of persons, restlessness, night wandering and visual hallucinations. It may be caused by hypoxia, due to various anaemias, or cardiovascular/circulatory and respiratory problems; drugs; trauma; metabolic disorders, including thyroid and liver diseases, hypo- and hyperglycaemia, hypo- and hypercalcaemia; infections; hypo- and hyperthermia; malnutrition; fluid/electrolyte

95

imbalance; and depression.[13] Acute brain syndrome is medically treatable and recovery can be complete if quickly recognised, assessed and treated.

Examples of potential nursing diagnoses

1 and 2   Sensory–perceptual alteration related to change in homoeostasis.

Potential nursing interventions

1   Assess source/origin of confusion.

- Establish communication; use direct eye contact and touch; check vital signs.
- Perform mental status questionnaire (MSQ) (see Chapter 2, 'Neurological system').
- Orient the person as to time and place if errors are made in the MSQ.
- Investigate hallucinations/areas of confusion for potential validity.
- Perform neurological, respiratory, and cardiac assessment.
- Check blood glucose level with a reagent strip.
- Evaluate recent history for: changes in medication, including any that have been discontinued; relocations; losses; environmental changes; and anything else that is out of the ordinary.
- Inform medical staff of the person's condition.

2   Implement reality orientation measures to reduce/resolve confusion.

- Acknowledge the reality of hallucinations to the person. For example, in the case of a visual hallucination, the nurse might say: 'I know that spiders are very frightening to you, but I can't see them.'
- Inform the person of where they are, who they are talking to, the time, day and date, and what has been happening.
- Avoid the use of restraints.
- Be aware of the potential problems with sedative/tranquillising drugs, should they be prescribed.
- Maintain a calm, quiet environment, in which noise is kept to an absolute minimum.

96

Chronic brain syndrome ('brain failure')

Chronic brain diseases have a gradual onset; their hallmark is dementia. This is chiefly characterised by intellectual deterioration, disorganisation of the personality, and the progressive inability to carry out the activities of daily living. Chronic brain diseases include multi-infarct dementia, Pick's disease, Huntington's chorea, Creutzfeld-Jakob disease, the dementias associated with syphilis and AIDS, and Alzheimer's disease.

Multi-infarct dementia probably accounts for about 20 per cent of the chronic brain disorders, and is due to diffuse cerebral arteriosclerosis. Symptoms are related to the amount and location of cortical damage.

Pick's disease, Huntington's chorea and Creutzfeld-Jakob disease are relatively rare dementias. In Pick's disease, the Pick cells located in the frontal portion of the cerebral cortex balloon and swell; progress of this disease is usually rapid, and symptoms closely resemble those of Alzheimer's disease. Huntington's chorea is characterised by manic mood changes and bizarre choreiform movements. Creutzfeld-Jakob disease is caused by a slow-growing virus that destroys cerebral tissue.

The dementia associated with untreated syphilis, sometimes referred to as tertiary syphilis, neurosyphilis or GPI ('general paralysis of the insane') is now very rare, antibiotic treatment of syphilis having been established over half a century; but the impact of AIDS on the older population has still to be properly assessed.

Alzheimer's disease ([senile] dementia of the Alzheimer type, SDAT, DAT) is the most prevalent dementia among older persons.[14] The underlying pathology of this disease is the development of neurofibrillary tangles and the accumulation of a plaque-like substance in the cerebral cortex that prevents the normal transmission/reception of stimuli. The exact cause is still unknown, but there is an associated decrease in a neurotransmitter known as choline acetyltransferase in the brain. No specific diagnostic test yet exists for this disease; medical diagnosis is made by ruling out other possible causes of signs and symptoms.[15]

The disease is generally characterised by four stages. The first is very insidious and generally lasts 2 to 4 years; symptoms include progressive forgetfulness, deterioration in short-term memory, and a progressive decline in the ability to do simple arithmetic. The person does not usually need specialised nursing care at this stage.

The second stage is marked by more pronounced forgetfulness. The person does not initiate normal routines and may forget to perform their usual hygiene practices. Speech becomes progressively slower and devoid of nouns. Disorientation to time and to day/night is also frequently seen in this stage. The person often becomes suspicious of everyone around him or her, and frequently voices unfounded (but often convincing) complaints of neglect or abuse. The course of this stage is variable; it may last years, or move rapidly into the third stage.

This is characterised by the development of ever more pronounced signs and symptoms. The affected person develops aphasia, agnosia (the inability to attach meaning to sensory impressions), and apraxia (the inability to carry out purposeful movement). The 'mirror sign', the inability to recognise one's own reflection, is noted, and the person may not recognise even close members of the family. Catastrophic reactions and uncontrolled behaviour that can include striking out and using abusive language, may also occur in this stage. Appetite may appear increased, but there is often weight loss.

The fourth, and final, stage is marked by even more pronounced deterioration. The person becomes incontinent, has marked weight loss, and has little or no response to stimuli. There may also be visual hallucinations and seizures.[16]

Nursing diagnoses and interventions depend upon the stage of the illness. The nursing assessment and history provide the basis for planning the nursing care, but priorities include:

1 Determine a method of communicating; establish which words the person uses for voiding, bowel elimination, pain, hunger and thirst. Determine if the person speaks more than one language.

2 Determine if the person recognises self and loved ones.

3 Determine which special senses are intact. A convenient method of assessing sight, hearing, motor control, and the ability to follow directions is the game SIMON™, or 'Simon Says'™, if you can find a toyshop that stocks it. This is a small electronic table game that produces four different sounds and colours in a random sequence; the object is to repeat the sequence by pressing the appropriate coloured panels. If this is not available, a similar game can be improvised.

4 Determine which ADLs the person can or cannot do for him/ herself.

Examples of potential nursing diagnoses

1 Alteration in thought processes related to inability to communicate.
2 Memory deficit associated with person, time and place.
3 Diversional activity deficit related to inactivity.
4 Sleep pattern disturbance due to not sleeping at night.
5 Potential for physical injury due to impaired judgement.
6 Alteration in nutrition, less than body requirements due to inability to eat.
7 Potential for fluid volume deficit due to inability to recognise thirst.
8 Alteration in bowel elimination, constipation due to toileting deficit.
9 Alteration in urinary elimination, incontinence.
10 Potential for violence related to impaired judgement.

Potential nursing interventions

1 Establish communication to reduce undesirable behaviour (specify).

- Stand directly in front of the person when communicating.
- Institute eye contact.
- Use touch when talking to the person.
- Use simple, short phrases.
- Do not argue with the person, but distract him or her with another activity.
- Stroke the person's face lightly upward and backward if he or she is noisy or disruptive.

2 Implement measures to maintain orientation (specify) – for example, assist the person with remembering where his or her bed/room is).

- Provide name sign on bed.
- Place familiar objects, pictures, and so on in the bed area or room.
- Repeat information frequently throughout the day.

3 Implement an activity programme consistent with the person's ability.

- Walk with the person (outside, if possible) every day.

- Involve in reminiscence; begin with an era appropriate for the person's age which is likely to have resonance for him or her.
- Have the person sort and identify old family photographs.

4 Modify activities to encourage sleeping at night.

- Plan activities early on in the day.
- Reduce activities after the evening meal. (*Note*: physical activities result in fatigue, which increases confusion.)
- Draw curtains, reduce lighting to a safe minimum to give cues/clues as to time at night.

5 Reduce potential for injury through modification of environment.

- Remove or tape over any privacy locks, if the person is occupying a room.
- Ensure that doors in the vicinity give some form of audible signal when opened.
- Ensure that the person has some form of identification on them at all times (in hospital, this could be a wrist band).
- Remove all objects that could be broken and thus become hazardous (for example, glassware).

6 Provide adequate nutrition to maintain/attain specified weight.

- Avoid all distracting influences at meal times, or as many as possible.
- Offer dishes singly.
- Remove unnecessary dishes and silverware from the tray.
- If the person cannot feed him- or herself, it may be necessary to give assistance.
- Offer snacks at specified times.

7 Maintain adequate hydration.

- Serve or provide a glass of fluid every 2–3 hours.
- Specify a beverage with meals.
- Monitor intake.

8 Prevent constipation.

- Maintain bowel record.

- Provide high fibre foods; add bran to cereals.
- See other measures listed in Chapter 6, under 'Constipation/faecal impaction'.

9   Implement measures to prevent incontinence.

- Place identifying sign on toilet/bathroom door.
- See other interventions listed in Chapter 5, 'Incontinence'.

10   Reduce the occurrence of catastrophic reactions.

- Observe for restlessness; restrict group activities if the person appears to be becoming agitated.
- Stop and distract the person, and remove to a quiet place, if control is, or is about to be, lost.

Normal pressure hydrocephalus

Normal pressure hydrocephalus (NPH) can be classified as either an acute or a chronic brain syndrome. The condition is characterised by dilation of the ventricles of the brain, stasis of the cerebrospinal fluid (CSF), and normal CSF pressure. People with this condition develop a scissors-like gait, sudden incontinence and confusion! NPH is usually diagnosed by CAT scan, and is treatable by the insertion of a shunt. Early detection is the key to the prevention of a chronic, irreversible brain syndrome being established.

Examples of potential nursing diagnoses and nursing interventions

See the sections relating to these throughout this chapter.

101

CHAPTER NINE

Health problems associated with vision and hearing

Perception is based on the functional ability of the elderly person's senses that influence behaviour; and sensory changes occur gradually with ageing. The purpose of this chapter is to provide the nurse with information to assist with developing nursing diagnoses and interventions in the area of health problems relating to vision and hearing, and with the promotion of the optimum use of remaining sensory function.

Vision

Glaucoma is one of the most serious eye diseases of older people; if untreated, total blindness will occur. A gradual loss of peripheral vision is an initial symptom; later ones include pain in either or both eyes, and the appearance of haloes around lights.

Cataracts are caused by opacification and degenerative diseases in the lens of the eye. Initially, there is often a marked improvement in the ability to read without glasses, but this is followed by blurred, dimmed vision. There are several methods of removing cataracts surgically, and the procedures are quick and simple. Contact lenses may be worn after some procedures, and the nurse needs to be aware of the different types available, and the proper removal and cleaning techniques for them.

Example of potential nursing diagnosis

1   Sensory – perceptual alteration related to decline in vision.

Potential nursing interventions

1 Plan and organise environment and personal space to accommodate visual loss.

- Plan placement of the person's personal effects, water jug and other significant objects with the person who has the sight impairment, and ensure that everyone is aware of the placement and that it should not be altered.
- At mealtimes place the food in a 'clock face' fashion, and inform the person where each type of food is located (for example peas at three o'clock, meat between five and nine, potatoes at eleven o'clock).
- Place the visually impaired person's hand on the caregiver's upper arm, and have the caregiver walk beside and fractionally ahead of the person when guiding/familiarising him or her with halls and stairs.
- Always explain exactly what is to happen, or what is to be done to the visually impaired person.
- Always make an audible signal and identify yourself before entering the person's room/bed area, and always inform the person when you are leaving.

Hearing

Age-related hearing loss (presbycusis) is common among older people, but it is by no means universal; and those individuals with mild hearing loss may have developed compensatory mechanisms that serve them very well indeed. The only certain way of assessing the degree of hearing loss is through audiometric testing. Additionally, there is an increased probability of impacted cerumen in the auditory canal, which interferes with hearing and can lead to infection.

Example of potential nursing diagnosis

1 Sensory – perceptual alteration related to hearing loss.

Potential nursing interventions

1 Facilitate communication.

- Always face the hearing-impaired person and speak slowly, in a low-toned voice.
- Use visual means of communication, such as gestures, cards, word lists.
- If the person has a hearing aid, ensure that the ear mould is kept clean, and that the connecting tubing is patent.
- Replace old batteries before the expiration date, if possible, and keep a record of the dates of changing.
- Arrange for audiometric testing, if necessary.

CHAPTER TEN

Metabolic disorders

Common health problems affecting the endocrine system may occur from a disturbance in the secretion of hormones. A *deficiency* in a specific hormone usually results from destruction of the gland, cancer, infection, or from inadequate stimulation. An *excess* is usually due to tumour, hyperplasia, or hypertrophy. The purpose of this chapter is to provide the nurse with potential nursing diagnoses and appropriate nursing interventions for patients or clients who are experiencing health problems of the endocrine system.

Diabetes mellitus

The peak age incidence of newly diagnosed diabetes mellitus is 60 to 70. Classic symptoms such as thirst, sweating, polyuria and tachycardia are often absent in the older person; behaviour disorders, confusion, nocturnal headache and slurred speech are usually the first symptoms. Decreased vision, intermittent claudication, numbing of the extremities, and shiny, hairless skin over the lower legs may also be indicative of diabetes mellitus. The renal threshold for glucose increases with age, and older people can be hyperglycaemic without sugar 'spilling over' into the urine.[1]

The condition is classified into two types: Type I, insulin-dependent diabetes mellitus (IDDM); and Type II, which is non-insulin dependent (NIDDM). Older people generally develop NIDDM, because the body cells are not receptive or sensitive to the insulin produced by the body, even though there may be what seems to be a sufficiency in the bloodstream.

Hypoglycaemia is usually a greater threat to older diabetics than hyperglycaemia, particularly if they are taking one of the longer-acting sulphonylurea drugs, or are using insulin. Additionally, they tend to develop hyperglycaemic hyperosmotic nonketotic coma (HHNK) rather than ketoacidosis when their diabetes goes out of control.

The primary focus of medical treatment is on the management of diet and medication. Recognition of the individual's idiosyncratic signs and symptoms of hypo- and hyperglycaemia is most important in order to gain control of their blood glucose balance.

Examples of potential nursing diagnoses

1 Potential for fluid volume deficit due to hyperosmolarity.
2 Alteration in nutrition, less than body requirements, related to inadequate glucose reaching the cells.
3 Potential for impairment of skin integrity due to compromised circulation.

Potential nursing interventions

1 Maintain adequate hydration.

- Assess skin for decreased turgor, observe mucous membranes for dryness.
- Offer and provide fluids frequently (minimum 1500 ml/day, medical considerations permitting).

2 Maintain adequate blood glucose levels.

- Administer the hypoglycaemic agent at the same time each day.
- If insulin mixtures are being used, do not prepare the injection until it is due to be given, unless a special, stabilised product has been prescribed.
- Rotate and record injection sites.
- Do not rely on urine sugar levels to provide accurate information about blood sugar levels, as the renal threshold may be altered, and the information they give may be some hours old.

3 Maintain skin integrity.

- Apply lanolin-based lotion or oil daily to the skin, and avoid problems of demoisturisation due to excessive bathing.
- Provide daily foot care, assessing skin condition each time.
- Arrange for chiropody, and ensure that staff do not attempt to cut the person's toenails themselves.

106

Hypothyroidism

Hypothyroidism is a common health problem of older people, and its development may be overlooked because the symptoms are not specific. Weakness, cold intolerance, memory impairment, weight gain, facial oedema, hair loss, dry skin, chest pain and constipation are amongst the commonest first manifestations; but each and every one of these may be put down to 'normal ageing' by some people.

Myxoedema coma, or profound hypothyroidism, is a medical emergency that requires skilled attention. Myxoedema often follows a serious illness, such as myocardial infarction, gastrointestinal bleeding, stroke, or infection; and again, symptoms can be misunderstood. Hypothermia is perhaps the commonest sign of abnormally low thyroxine levels.[2] Medical diagnosis is made through blood testing, and the treatment is simply thyroxine replacement.

Examples of potential nursing diagnoses

1 Alteration in cardiac output due to decreased heart rate.
2 Alteration in sensory perception, related to coldness.

Potential nursing interventions

1 Monitor closely for vascular collapse.

- Monitor heart rate and rhythm, blood pressure.
- Auscultate heart, chest sounds for development of pericardial, pleural effusions.

2 Keep the person warm, avoid chilling.

- Monitor temperature.
- Avoid the use of heating pads, electric blankets, which may warm too rapidly.
- Provide extra clothing, blankets; encourage the wearing of woollen leg-warmers.

Hyperthyroidism

Hyperthyroidism is less common than hypothyroidism among older people, but it is a health problem that is similarly often overlooked. People with this condition often complain of fatigue, leg cramps, palpitations, nervousness and heat intolerance. Weight loss, exophthalmos (protrusion of the eyes), elevated temperature and cardiac arrhythmias are frequently noted. Clinical manifestations of hyperthyroidism may be less obvious in older patents, in whom it may surface as arrhythmia and cardiac failure.[3]

Diagnosis is by laboratory testing, and medical treatment is aimed at suppressing thyroid function/production.

Examples of potential nursing diagnoses

1 Alteration in nutrition, less than body requirements, due to increased metabolism.
2 Potential for eye injury due to protrusion of the eyes.
3 Alteration in cardiac output due to increased rate.

Potential nursing interventions

1 Maintain adequate nutrition, body weight.

- Increase number of meals and snacks.
- Weigh weekly, at the same time of day, and using the same scales

2 Protect eyes from corneal damage, injury.

- Encourage use of dark glasses if the person is exposed to bright light, particularly sunlight.
- If eyelids do not close completely, apply protective patches during the night.
- Instil drops as ordered.

3 Monitor for increased cardiac workload.

- Assess vital signs, including temperature.
- Keep the environment as cool as possible.
- Apply cool compresses to the forehead if the person finds the ambient temperature too high.
- Do not give aspirin as an antipyretic, as it increases thyroxine levels.[4]

CHAPTER ELEVEN

Skin disorders

The major function of the skin is protective. Other functions include heat regulation, sensation and body image. Gradual changes occur in the skin of the older person, especially the surfaces exposed to environmental and (less importantly for residents of the British Isles) solar trauma. A common health problem involving the integumentary system of the older person is often the development of decubitus ulcers (decubiti, pressure- or bed-sores). The purpose of this chapter is to guide the nurse to possible interventions for patients or clients with the nursing diagnoses of alteration in skin integrity, actual or potential. One guiding principle worth bearing in mind throughout what follows is this: You can put almost anything you like on a pressure sore – except the patient.

Decubitus ulcers

The immobile older person is a high-risk candidate for the development of pressure sores due to fragility of the skin, decreased blood supply, reduced pressure sensation and poor nutrition. There is only one truly effective way of dealing with such sores, and that is prevention.

Identification of those individuals who are apt to develop pressure sores is the first step in prevention. There are several tried and tested 'at risk' scoring systems, the most familiar of which are probably those developed by Norton[1] and Waterlow.[2]

There are many different types of pressure-relieving mattresses (such as the 'Nimbus' and 'Pegasus' types) and cushions (for example, the 'Roho' or oil-filled models) available for use, if the budget can stretch to these; but it must never be forgotten that these are *aids* to pressure-area care, not solutions to the problem.

109

The skin must be kept scrupulously clean and dry, but care must be taken not to demoisturise it. Soap with a high fat content is useful, as are various moisturising preparations.

Immobile or bedfast persons must be turned and repositioned frequently to prevent pressure damage. People sitting in wheelchairs, or on any relatively hard seat, need to be repositioned more frequently, due to the unequal distribution of their body weight. An individual, written schedule can be helpful in ensuring consistent pressure relief. All pressure areas should be checked at turning times.

If nursing 'care' has failed, and the skin has broken, there is no time to waste. Assessment of the broken area or ulcer is the first step in the healing protocol. Byrne and Feld suggest suggest classifying sores into four stages:[3]

Stage I: The epidermis and dermis are damaged, but not destroyed.

Stage II: The epidermis and dermis are destroyed, and damage has reached the subcutaneous layer.

Stage III: The subcutaneous layer has been destroyed, and there is cavity formation.

Stage IV: Muscle and bone tissue are involved, and skin tissues and structures are decayed.

Written records, diagrams and, whenever possible, photographs of any lesions are invaluable when it comes to evaluating treatment. Swabs for culture and sensitivity should be sent from all wounds, particularly in the hospital setting, where the wound may have been colonised by resistant organisms such as MRSA (methicillin-resistant staphylococcus aureus).

A wide variety of decubitus ulcer treatments are available, from simple occlusive dressings, through hydrocolloids and absorbent agents, to combinations of different types, enzymatic desloughing agents and a wide variety of others which appear with regularity on the market, each promising advances on everything that has gone before. The important issue in the nursing management of pressure sores is that the treatment is selected for research-based reasons, used consistently, and properly evaluated; with the emergence of specialist wound-care journals, there is no excuse for ignorance of the latest recommendations.

It is every nurse's duty, under the Code of Conduct,[4] parts 1, 2 and 3, to keep her patients from harm, and to offer the best possible care; there is a strong argument for claiming that the development of a pressure sore is evidence of failure in itself, in this regard. The treatment of sores is similarly guided by the Code; it is essential that we know *what* we are doing, and *why*, when dressing a wound of any description. This includes being as up-to-date as possible in our knowledge of available treatments, including their drawbacks.

Stasis ulcers

Although the development of leg ulcers is due to chronic arterial or venous insufficiency, secondary to cardiac problems or solely to peripheral vascular disease, it is discussed in this section rather than with the cardiovascular diseases because the chief nursing concern is with impaired skin integrity. Like pressure sores, they are easier to prevent than to cure, and they require intensive nursing management.

Stasis ulcers are the result of chronic impairment of blood flow to or from the feet. Ulcers are usually, though not always, located on the inner aspect of the ankle when the impairment is due to chronic venous insufficiency. The surrounding skin has a brown discoloration, and may be inflamed; this condition is known as stasis dermatitis. The foot becomes cyanotic when lowered, and any pain is not usually severe.[5]

When the ulcer is due to chronic arterial insufficiency, it is usually seen on the lateral areas of the ankle or shin; the toes and feet may also be involved. The surrounding skin is pale and shiny, and redness results when the foot is lowered; pain is almost always severe.[6]

The first step in the management of stasis ulcers is assessment and, as mentioned under 'Decubitus ulcers' above, photographs can be invaluable. Full written records must be maintained; pulses and the colour of the extremity are recorded.

The area must be protected from any injury; bed cradles and other aids must be used to avoid pressure and shearing from bed linen.

For recommendations on wound care, see the preceding section; there is a multitude of different dressings for leg ulcers on the market, and by the time this book goes to press, the number will have increased. An adjunct to all these, however, is that for venous ulcers, some form of compression bandaging is used to assist venous

111

return in the limb. This means that a very careful check of the circulation in the affected area must be maintained. In the case of arterial ulcers, compression will rapidly exacerbate tissue damage, perhaps irremediably.

PART III

Focusing on the whole person

CHAPTER TWELVE

Psychosocial aspects of care
BRIAN BOOTH, RGN

Introduction

*Why 'psychosocial'? Why not 'Mental health – aspects of care'?
Nursing has enough jargon, surely; do we really need any more?*

*'Psychosocial' is not an attractive word, certainly, but it is becoming
popular – because it describes something for which no-one has, as yet,
come up with an acceptable alternative term. When we, as nurses, use
the nursing process (described in the introduction to Part II as being
made up of assessment, diagnosis, planning, implementing and
evaluating care), we do not look at the patient or client as a purely
biological construction. Yet it is not all that long ago that many nurses
did just that; readers who practised before the mid-1980s will
remember hearing people referred to as, say, 'the appendix in bed
3','the chest by the window', 'the MI in the sideroom', and so on. In
addition to the person's body, we are conscious of both psychological
and social aspects of their life. The RSCN on the paediatric medical
ward, faced with a malnourished child, does not see the beginning and
end of her job as getting sufficient calories into that child to reach
some predetermined desired age/height/weight ratio; nor would she
consider the problem 'solved' if organic causes were ruled out, leaving
a simple answer of 'increase intake' for the parents to take away with
them.*

*At the other end of the age spectrum, no elderly-care nurse worthy
of the name sees her patients or clients as mere biologically
malfunctioning units. The phrase 'holistic care' is bandied about as
though it were something new, but when John Donne wrote, nearly
four centuries ago, 'No man is an island', he was saying that each
individual is inextricably bound up in a greater whole, which he called
'mankind'.[1] If we replace that word with 'society', the discussion comes*

down from the rarefied air of metaphysics, to land squarely in the real world that we all inhabit.

Think of all the older people in whose care you have been professionally involved; can you remember a single person for whom 'social factors' were considered irrelevant? Did it matter whether or not they lived alone? Did the type of housing have to be ascertained before discharge was planned? Was there any need to think about whether or not anyone would be visiting them at home? Could their family be left out of care planning – and if there was no family, did that have any bearing on discharge planning?

Whatever organic problem has led to an older person needing nursing care, anyone involved in the planning of that care must take social factors into consideration; but when there is any perceived psychological dysfunction, these factors come to the fore, as we shall see in the rest of this chapter. And that is why the word 'psychosocial' appears in the title; for it is the author's belief that the way older people fit into society has profound implications for the planning of care.

* * *

Negative expectations of ageing are rife in British society; and as we are part of that society, we cannot really claim to be different – just better informed. A simple test of attitudes, well worth undertaking, is to ask any number of health-care workers, preferably from a wide range of specialities and varied experience, a few questions.

It is easy enough to make up your own but for example, you might ask: (a) what percentage of people over the age of 65, roughly, suffer with dementia?; (b) what percentage of this age group is in some form of long-term care setting?, and (c) what would you think if an 85-year-old told you that they were sexually active?

From the author's experience, the sorts of answers to be expected are along the following lines: (a) Anything from 50 to 90 per cent, with very few people estimating much below that; (b) Anything from 20 to 75 per cent; and (c) A wide range of responses, which might include disgust, or sheer disbelief that such a thing might be possible. (As a matter of interest, the answers to the first two are 5–8 per cent[2] and 5 per cent[3] respectively; there is no 'correct' answer to the third, of course, but there is no reason at all for an older person to cease sexual relations, unless they are too ill – which applies equally to an 18-year old.)

The problem with negative expectations is that they can very easily become self-fulfilling prophecies.[4] A person who has reached the age of

116

eighty, say, with no significant current health problems, has to get used to hearing 'You've done well – aren't you lucky!', with its tacit assumption that everyone's luck runs out, sooner or later. And should that person need nursing care, it is not unusual for it to be said 'Ah well, at that age, what can you expect?' – even if the reason for needing that care is unrelated to age or general health, such as trauma. It is true to say that there is a large number of people over retirement age who need medical or nursing intervention at some point; but given society's expectations, it is a wonder that the number is not larger.

* * *

'But in this world nothing can be said to be certain, except death and taxes,' wrote Benjamin Franklin. In the twentieth century, with its generally higher life expectancies, Western society seems to have added '. . . and dementia'. We seem to have forgotten that the words 'senile' and 'Senator' have the same root; and certainly, many elderly-care nurses can attest to the fact that when they tell anyone what their job is, there is often an assumption on the listener's part that the person is spending their days in the company of people who have parted company with reality. Any attempt to correct this idea, by giving examples of the wide variety of subjects on which her patients or clients have informed her over the years, is likely to be met with disbelief – and the oddest part about it is, sometimes it is people who are themselves classed as 'elderly' who make these assumptions.

It seems that many people have mistaken increased probability for absolute certainty. As the body ages, as we saw in Part II, it becomes increasingly likely that it will not function as well as it once did; as the saying goes, life is a sexually-transmitted disease, with a 100 per cent mortality rate. The ageing process starts in the twenties, and continues until death; the process can be slowed a little, it is claimed, but it cannot be stopped. The same is not true of the mind, though it is, on the whole, where the brain is concerned. Yet even here, it is a matter of degree. If you think about the amount of learning that you did as an adolescent, does it seem likely that you could undertake that again, now, whatever your age? Probably not, if you are past your mid-twenties;[5] but when it comes to learning from experience, it is a different thing again.

The 80-year old's memory will not be as good as it was when the person was 20;[6] but then, neither will their renal function.[7] The probability of having developed an organic brain disorder, such as dementia of the Alzheimer's type, is much higher at 80 than at 40 – but not infinitely so.

117

The probability that the person will suffer some form of depression is very much higher, again, for the person of 80, when compared with someone of 40; but is this because the brain is 'failing', or could there be another reason? Leaving aside for the moment the theory that depression is caused purely by a chemical imbalance in the brain, and thinking of it as the natural response for some people to intolerable stress, consider the relative chances of a 40-year-old and an 80-year-old person having to face up to:

- *deaths of people close to them;*
- *worry about their own impending death;*
- *loss of income;*
- *loss of status;*
- *feelings of not being valued;*
- *feelings of not being able to contribute anything worthwhile to society;*
- *fear of falling ill, possibly mentally;*
- *feelings of isolation;*
- *belief that other people are finding them less and less attractive; and*
- *concerns about personal safety, in a world that seems to be increasingly violent.*

Either person could have to deal with any or all of the above; but for whom is it most likely? How many items on this list are connected with the way that our society treats the older person?

In what follows, we shall look at some of the commonest problems of mental health experienced by the elderly. A review of the available literature gives the impression that for many authors, particularly medical ones, ageing and mental dysfunction are somehow inseparable. It seems very easy, when reading these sorts of texts, to fall into the trap of thinking that there is not much to look forward to – 'second childishness, and mere oblivion, Sans teeth, Sans eyes, sans taste, sans everything'.[8]

Is there anyone better placed than nurses, when it comes to correcting these false impressions?

Classification

There is no doubt that classification systems are useful. In the introduction to Part II, we saw how the formulation of nursing diagnoses can assist with planning interventions more logically, and that communication is enhanced by the elimination of ambiguous terms. However, when we look at mental health problems in the elderly, it soon becomes apparent that classification also has its difficulties.

It is easy to forget how new the branch of medicine known as 'psychiatry' really is,[9] and as for 'psychogeriatrics' – the term is barely thirty years old.[10] Table 12.1 lists the headings used in classifying the disorders with which psychogeriatrics is concerned, and these are the terms that are used in the majority of textbooks; but it is worth bearing in mind that they can hardly be said to have proven historical value, which might make them indispensable.

Table 12.1

---

1 Mental illnesses
   (a) Organic
      (i) Delirium (acute confusional state)
     (ii) Dementia (chronic confusional state)
   (b) Functional
      (i) Affective illness: depression, mania
     (ii) Paranoid states
    (iii) Neuroses

2 Personality and behaviour disorders

Reprinted from: Pitt, B. 1982. *Psychogeriatrics – An Introduction to the Psychiatry of Old Age* (2nd edn). Edinburgh: Churchill Livingstone, 28.

The commonest place for an elderly-care nurse to find such problems so neatly defined is in the textbooks; in the real world, things are rarely so cut-and-dried. We are back with probabilities again. As we have seen, in the process of normal ageing, the chances of the body going wrong in one way or another is increasing all the time. So, for example, there is a good chance that a 70-year old person in Britain will be taking medication of some sort, prescribed by their GP; the altered muscle/fat/water ratio of the ageing body, in tandem with a less efficient renal system, leads to an increased probability of those drugs not being eliminated from the body as completely as they would have been some years earlier; and the build up could lead to a toxic state that affects mental functioning.

There is no end of examples. An underactive thyroid can lead to a person entering a paranoid state;[11] drugs used for the treatment of Parkinson's disease may cause hallucinations.[12] Lurid accounts in the media of elderly people being beaten and robbed could frighten some individuals into a state where they will not answer the door or

119

go out unaccompanied; high food costs, coupled with an excess of financial prudence, might have the consequence for some people of malnutrition and an associated clouding of consciousness . . . readers experienced in elderly care will be able to extend the list indefinitely.

So, a potential problem of classification is this: *any older person who presents with symptoms that seem to fit the standard definitions of mental disorder, is more likely than a younger person to have a completely different problem altogether* – and possibly, more than one. And even if they *do* have such a disorder, there is a high probability of other, complicating factors being present. They may be victims of Alzheimer's disease, and have a high blood glucose level, or a urinary tract infection, or be depressed, at the same time.

The labels in Table 12.1 have their uses; but nurses must treat them with caution. If it is forgotten that 'dementia' is not a disease, but merely a convenient shorthand term for a group of symptoms, it becomes easy to slip into a way of thinking that lumps all people with the same diagnosis together; the first sign of this is when we start planning care for the medical diagnosis, and not the person.

Delirium (acute confusional state)

Delirium is defined by one psychologist as 'a grossly disordered state of brain function characterised by restlessness, incoherent speech, and delusions . . . [it] is, as a rule, of toxic origin'.[13] When you consider that this condition could be caused by a subdural haematoma, in which the level of consciousness might be lowered, or by an episode of cerebral ischaemia, which cannot be described as a toxic state, it can be seen that the term 'delirium' is not a helpful one - hence the more common use of 'acute confusional state'. (Another term, which might one day enter common usage, is 'reversible dementia',[14] but this has its own problems: is a confusional state due to an operable brain tumour to be classed differently from one where the growth is inoperable? Also, the layman's understanding of the word 'dementia' could lead to misapprehensions in discussions with medical staff.)

Acute confusional states are, on the whole, easily treatable, but everything depends on the rapid and accurate identification of the underlying cause; and everyone involved in care needs skill, knowledge and patience in large quantities.

One of the key factors in differentiating such states from true dementia lies in determining the time period over which the symptoms appeared (as a very rough rule of thumb, less than 48 hours, as opposed to the weeks and months of being demented; in the United States, this period is seen as diagnostic). In Britain, many elderly people live alone; some of them may not see other people for long periods, except the counter staff in shops and post offices (such staff are very good at picking up problems, particularly in the smaller establishments); increasing confusion may not be noted for some time, if at all. If the cause is something like a 'silent' myocardial infarction, the person may not even look unwell. By the time their GP has been alerted, or an emergency admission through A & E has proved necessary, the person may have become unkempt and malnourished, possibly even incontinent. For the assessing practitioner, who may not know anything about the person, a diagnosis of 'dementia' is all too easy to make, particularly if no physical disorders are apparent. Even if there is an overt health problem, such as like a respiratory or urinary tract infection, the confused state can persist for days or weeks after the resolution of that problem.

If health-care workers have mistaken beliefs about the prevalence of mental disorder in the elderly, there is a high probability that some of their patients or clients may be treated as though they had a chronic, irremediable problem, rather than one which was acute and reversible – and as mentioned above, self-fulfilling prophecies can be made.

In Chapter 1, great stress was laid on the importance of gathering as much information as possible about anyone for whom we are to plan care; some readers may have wondered how necessary it really is to go into such detail. In the case of acute confusional states, the importance of physical *and social* assessment cannot be overstressed; a less than thorough assessment could, for some people, mean the difference between the resolution of a temporary psychological disturbance, and the induction of a permanent one.

Dementia (chronic confusional state)

Of the nine million or so British residents over the age of 65, it has been estimated that between 5 and 8 per cent suffer from some form of dementia.[15] If only 'moderate to severe' dementia is considered, the figure falls to somewhere between 1.3 and 6.2 per cent.[16] The probability of occurrence rises with age: after the age of 80, the texts seem to agree, incidence rises to between 20 and 22 per cent. So, as life expectancy rises, so does the absolute number of people diagnosed as having some form of this condition, be it of the Alzheimer type, multiple cerebral infarct, or whatever.

At the same time, British society is changing. Compared to only fifty years ago, families have fewer children; and despite the good intentions of successive governments, 'community care' still means 'family care' – which, as experienced readers will know, falls chiefly on daughters (and daughters-in-law).[17] Divorce and remarriage are much more common; and, it was estimated in 1990 that two-thirds of all women aged between 35 and 54 held down some sort of job.[18]

At the same time, continuing-care beds are disappearing from the NHS, as the private sector grows; in 1987, a survey showed that over half of all elderly care beds were in private nursing homes, and there is no reason to doubt that the proportion is increasing.[19]

What has all this to do with planning care for older people with chronic confusional states? Consider the following true story from the author's recent experience, in which only names have been changed.

Mrs Rolls, an 87-year-old lady, lived alone in a warden-controlled flat. One day she fell, fracturing the neck of her left femur; this was successfully repaired, and she was transferred to a rehabilitation ward for mobilisation and preparation for discharge.

It was obvious that Mrs Rolls was in the early stages of dementia of the Alzheimer's type; her daughter, Barbara, confirmed that her mother's memory had been slowly worsening for some years, but recently she had started expressing paranoid thoughts. Physical rehabilitation proceeded without problems, with Mrs Rolls rapidly becoming independent with a Zimmer frame, and her heart failure was very well controlled on digoxin.

It was apparent from the outset that there would be difficulties with her discharge. Because of her mental state, she was at risk of injuring herself and others; she was quite likely to light a cigarette and forget about it, or allow pans to boil dry. In addition, her flat was on the first floor; the block had just been bought by a private company, and although her reasonably low rent was protected at the moment, there was a good chance that if she moved into the ground-floor flat that had just become vacant, that rent would almost double.

Barbara simply could not afford to give up her job to spend more time with her mother, as this was a time of high interest rates, and she needed every penny to put towards mortgage payments. There was no question of her taking Mrs Rolls to live with her, as Barbara had remarried, and her new husband was already voicing objections to Barbara's son and daughter-in-law possibly moving in with them. (This son was due to come out of the army, but there were no council flats available in the area without several years' wait, all the best housing having been sold off; so there was nowhere else that he and his wife could go, while they saved towards a place of their own.)

Barbara's brother, David, wanted his mother to go into some form of long-term care – but only if he did not have to contribute towards the cost. With no children, and a very large house, it was thought that perhaps he would consider taking his mother in, but he would not countenance this; he felt strongly that it was 'a woman's (that is, Barbara's) job', yet as the only son, he insisted that the final say in any plans should be his.

The nursing staff were beginning to feel that everyone was being considered except Mrs Rolls herself, and felt very strongly that if she went anywhere other than back to her own home, her mental condition would deteriorate rapidly. All the stops were pulled out in trying to organise domiciliary care; but the Social Services department, at the end of the financial year and in the throes of a national reorganisation, simply did not have the money to pay for what they felt to be the minimum level of support, and the community nursing services were under so much pressure that they declined to even guess at how much input they could provide.

Barbara reduced her hours at work; the social worker negotiated a minimal rent rise for Mrs Rolls in the ground floor flat, and took an immense risk by providing home carers whose regular clients were in hospital, praying that none would be discharged before the new financial year started. And so Mrs Rolls went home.

Five days later, she was readmitted after a fall, which she could not remember happening.

In the 1930s, it would have been unlikely that someone with Mrs Rolls' cardiac condition would have lived to be 87; and if she had, there may well have been more than two children and one grandchild, all of whom would probably have accepted it as their 'duty' to care for her, at whatever inconvenience to themselves. The family was also quite likely to live in a geographically small area, rather than be spread out.

These are the sorts of changes that are having such a profound effect on the way care is being planned for an increasingly elderly population; any reader who wishes to look further into this subject is advised to have a look at T. Dartington's book, *The Limits of Altruism*.[20] British society has to face up to the problems that changing demography will bring in the next few decades, and elderly care specialists should be in the vanguard. Who else has such close contact with the people who will need to use the available services, and their families? Who else is better able to point out that, just possibly, it is not 'the elderly' who are the problem?

Affective illness: depression

In the introduction to this chapter, we saw ten examples of reasons why older people may become 'depressed'; there was also a suggestion that at least some of these were directly related to the attitudes of society as a whole. But just how widespread is depression amongst the elderly?

Several surveys[21] generated the much-quoted estimate of 1.8 to 2.5 per cent of over-65s suffering from 'severe depressive psychoses'; but when it comes to the 'milder' conditions, difficulties arise because of the ambiguity in the very word 'depression'. Any textbook dealing with the subject will give the interested reader more information; but to demonstrate the scale of the problem, one study found that 70 per cent of over-65s had occasional depressive preoccupations,[22] while another said that of this whole age group, only 13 per cent would be depressed to the point where health was affected.[23] It has been suggested that there is a lesser form of depression in the elderly, which its describers called 'dysphoric syndrome'.[24]

The good response of so many older people to antidepressant drugs has led to theorising that the condition may be purely biochemical; but on the whole, studies have tended to conclude that certain neurotransmitter changes associated with ageing are *predisposing*, rather than *causative* factors.[25] Much more important, it seems, is the individual's lifelong overall personality, when it comes to discussing why the life crises that precipitate deep depression in one person are shrugged off by another.[26]

Old age seems to many of us to be characterised by loss; unless prompted, we do not readily think of the gains (such as experience, the chance to see a third or fourth generation, leisure to do whatever one wants, freedom from responsibility, and so on).[27] Loss of family and friends, loss of status, loss of income, loss of health (and with that, loss of independence) – for the old, some of us seem to think, there is not much to be gained by living.

Loss is a virtually inescapable part of ageing; only those who die young have a chance of escaping it. Yet it may be one of the *gains* of advancing years, the accumulated experience that enables people to cope with inevitable losses. If there were no truth in that, why is the incidence of depression in the elderly so far below 100 per cent?

Perhaps the importance of loss has been overemphasised by writers handicapped by relative youth, and thus lacking the essential first-hand experience, at the expense of 'learned helplessness'.[28] Many, though by no means all, the textbooks dealing with depression mention this concept, in greater or lesser detail. Very briefly, the underlying principle (which comes from animal psychology, possibly affecting its credibility amongst professionals used to dealing with real, live people) is that when nothing one does has any effect, then the tendency is to give up altogether. If a rat in a box is given electric shocks through the floor, when standing on one half of it, it rapidly learns to stand in the other half. If shocks are administered there, too, the poor animal might not, as could be expected, try returning to the other half, to see if that is any better, but just freezes; it is as though it is thinking 'What's the point?'. Seligman, who developed the concept of learned helplessness, suggested that this 'attitude' was directly analogous to depression in humans: if someone feels that they are no longer the captains of their fate, then they may as well go down with the ship. Any reader who has had the misfortune to work in a task-oriented psychogeriatric ward in the past will understand this instantly; for when someone is not allowed to even attempt dressing or feeding themselves, because there is 'no time', it is not usually long before they slip into a totally passive state. Some individuals may be roused enough to fight the system for a while, but chemical treatment of 'agitation' has the same effect in the end.

If society as a whole has no interest in hearing the views of the elderly, then with a few vocal and unrepresentative exceptions, the elderly may just shut up, or retreat into talking to themselves; if someone asks for the same respect which they honestly believe they once paid to their elders and betters, and do not get it, they may come to believe that they are unworthy of respect; if attempts to maintain a positive self-image which differs from society's expect-ations are met with derision ('mutton dressed as lamb', 'Jogging? At his age, you'd think he'd know better'), then it is no surprise if those attempts are eventually given up.

Say something loud enough, and for long enough, and at least some people will come to believe it. Has British society been saying that the over-65s are silly, sexless old fools? If it has, perhaps no-one should be surprised to learn that in this 12 per cent of the population, more than a third of all successful suicide attempts are made.[29]

Paranoid states

True paranoia, which is characterised by an unshakeable belief that the person is being harassed or persecuted in some way, is relatively rare in older people – about one per cent[30] – and is sometimes associated with an acute confusional state, disappearing when the underlying health problem is successfully treated. This persistent condition, sometimes referred to as paraphrenia, varies in its severity: one psychiatrist has described three distinct categories.[31]

Paraphrenia usually responds well to drug therapy – but how does one get the sufferer, who does not believe that there is anything wrong with him or her, to take the prescribed medication? (If the condition takes the form of believing that someone is trying to poison them, the problems are multiplied.) A compulsory treatment order under the 1983 Mental Health Act is one way; but is forcibly bringing a paranoid person into 'the asylum' such a good idea? But never mind about *their* rights; what about the rights of the people unjustly being accused of persecuting them?

Over the years, older people whom the author has nursed have said often that once upon a time everyone was more tolerant of bizarre behaviour in their neighbours; but seeing the way in which some of these same people have reacted to mentally disturbed patients on the same ward gives cause to wonder just how true this really is. When extended families were more commonplace, and generations were born in the same house, moving no more than a few streets away on getting married, perhaps there really was more tolerance; if so, does this mean that the changing picture of British urban life (and rural life, in the more picturesque parts) will lead to more paraphrenic people being subjected to compulsory treatment, under the pressure of local public opinion?[32]

Neuroses

'[A] neurosis is a habit that is . . . maladaptive in some obvious respect'[33] 'Neurosis means much the same as the lay term 'nerves': a tendency to get overwrought'.[34] The author was taught a useful way

126

of distinguishing neurosis from psychosis: neurotics build castles in the air; psychotics live in them (and psychiatrists collect the rent).

One thing is lacking from all these definitions: the fact that a neurotic person really *can* suffer. A psychosomatic pain is no less real for having no organic cause; and anyone who has nursed an elderly person with a severe neurotic disorder has seen the trembling and the sweating start and felt the sheer *terror* that is exuded, and will not treat the term 'neurosis' lightly again.

The diagnosis of 'neurotic disorder' is comparatively rare in older people. One pychogeriatrician has asked 'Is this because neurosis is actually less common, or because doctors get used to their ageing neurotics, and do not notice the onset of neurosis in old age?'[35] No one seems to have answered his question, so far.

It is all too easy to treat even severe neurosis as something barely to be taken seriously; doctors and nurses alike have been known to use phrases like 'don't be silly', 'pull yourself together' and so on – phrases that they would not dream of using to a person with a physical disability that limited their independence. Is this, perhaps, another manifestation of the 'silly old fool' mentality? Whatever the reason, it seems fair to assume that a great deal of suffering has resulted from intolerance of 'neurotic' behaviour – an adjective that has passed from precise psychological use into common parlance as a pointed insult.

Personality and behaviour disorders

A cynic might say that this is a catch-all title for anything that cannot be shoe-horned into one of the other categories; and a brief skim through some of the texts can reinforce this view. However, there is at least one common factor: all 'behaviour disorders', and most 'personality disorders', are not conditions that particularly distress the person in whom they have been diagnosed. (This is not to say that in some cases, the person cannot be seen to be 'suffering', compared to how they *could* be living.) Senile squalor ('Diogenes') syndrome;[36] miserliness; hoarding; exhibitionism; extreme stubbornness; urination in inappropriate places – unlike severe depression or neurosis – would not be 'problems' if the person lived on a desert island. But not many older people live on desert islands – although they may inhabit an island of loneliness, not necessarily by choice.

The whole category is, by its very nature, too broad to be discussed here; the interested reader is referred to Chapter 11 of Pitt's excellent book.[37]

Potential nursing diagnoses

Almost by definition, psychosocial problems are never simple. Whereas a nursing diagnosis of, say, 'potential for infection' is easily comprehended, and possible nursing interventions spring almost automatically to mind, a problem defined as 'spiritual distress' may not always lend itself to objective analysis. *Who* and *what* we are can have an effect on how we plan care in this sphere of practice, and we may even pass judgements on other people's fitness to do so – should a nurse who does not believe in a supreme being be allowed to work in a hospice, say, or is a person who has suffered with some form of mental illness fit to be employed in the mental health field? These are not questions of mere academic interest, but examples from real life; we shall return to this point later.

Table 12.2 lists some nursing diagnoses that can be made.

Table 12.2 *Potential nursing diagnoses*

Anxiety*
Impaired verbal communication
Ineffective individual coping*
Diversional activity deficit
Fear*
Alterations in family processes and ineffective family coping*
Grieving*
Powerlessness*
Disturbance in self-concept; body image, self esteem and role
    performance*
Sensory–perceptual impairment
Sleep pattern disturbance
Social isolation*
Spiritual distress*
Alterations in thought processes
Potential for violence*
Knowledge deficit*

* See text for explanation.

It is obvious that several of these headings imply some sort of subjectivity; one man's social isolation is another man's idea of heaven, for example. But as the development of diagnostic categories continues, it is to be hoped that the vagueness of definition which currently seems to be a feature of 'psychosocial problems' will lessen, enabling more objective and precise planning of nursing care.

A more complete list can be found in 'DSM-III',[38] a source of much of the material found in American textbooks; and McConnell's comprehensive discussion of eleven specific diagnoses (marked * in Table 12.2), being rooted firmly in nursing process-based practice, is a good starting point for readers who wish to see how nursing diagnoses can be translated into actual care.[39]

Conclusion

The whole area of 'psychosocial aspects of care' raises many more questions than answers; for unlike the majority of physical dysfunctions, psychological disturbances do not lend themselves to a simple 'identify cause and then treat' approach. If anyone came to this chapter to find answers, the author hopes that they will accept his apologies; for if answers that could be put down on paper exist, he has no idea where they are to be found. The best we can hope for at the present is some sight of signposts in the fog.

The basis of effective nursing care could be summarised as 'understand the person, and you will understand their problems'. There is not much room for argument there, when the problem is a fractured rib, but when it is a fractured psyche . . . .

Before we presume to interfere with people's innermost beings, perhaps we ought to ask ourselves how much we know about our own; a lack of self-awareness is no help in improving one's own nursing practice, particularly where attitudes are concerned. If we believe that growing old is a matter of slipping down a greasy biological pole towards inevitable decrepitude, then our ability to nurse older people is handicapped. Ageing is the one thing that all mankind has in common, and quite a few of us are going to need the services of elderly-care nurses in the future. In our own self-interest, if for nothing else, it is worth making sure that the practitioner of the future is both knowledgeable and effective; one way of doing that is to start doing our best *now* towards seeing that they do not think of older people as embarrassing, unwanted remainders of our society, but as a vibrant and essential part of it.

CHAPTER THIRTEEN

Nutrition

As age increases, the amount of calories needed to maintain health decreases. The current recommended intake in the United Kingdom is, for men aged 65 to 74, 2400 kcal (10MJ), falling to 2150 (9MJ) from the age of 75; for women, the equivalents are 1900 kcal (8MJ), and 1680 (7MJ).[1]

About 1g of protein per kg of body weight is required for the maintenance of body systems. For an older person, 10 per cent to 12 per cent of total caloric intake should come from protein, while carbohydrates should make up about 80 per cent. The exact figure is determined by the recommendations on fat intake, which has been a contentious issue in recent years. American nutritionists feel that fat should make up about 10 per cent of the caloric total,[2] but some British writers have pointed out that for the older person who is eating less, fats provide energy over a longer period than do carbohydrates,[3] in a lower total volume.[4] This topic seems certain to be debated for some years to come.

However, illnesses, both acute and chronic, and injury alter nutritional requirements, as additional calories and protein are needed for repair and maintenance of body systems during illness and disease.

Major sources of protein are meat, fish, eggs, milk and milk products; major sources of carbohydrates are sugars and starches, including those found in grains, fruit and vegetables, which are the ideal for older people. The chief sources of fat are animal fats, butter and plant oils, the latter having become increasingly popular in Britain in recent years. As we have noted, there is a great deal of controversy surrounding fat intake; the relationship between this and atherosclerosis is still far from being definitively established, research on the advantages of a fat-modified or cholesterol-lowering diet still being awaited.

In addition to fats, protein and carbohydrates, attention must be paid to the vitamin and mineral contents of the older person's diet. One very important mineral is calcium, but here, too, there is dispute. One group of researchers claimed that there was a definite relationship between osteoporosis and low calcium intake,[5] whilst others questioned this assertion.[6] However, there is no doubt whatsoever that debilitated people are at greatest risk for developing accelerated osteoporosis, and it has been recommended that post-menopausal women who are not taking oestrogen need 1500mg of calcium daily as a prophylactic measure.[7] In addition to decreased calcium intake, the efficiency of its absorption declines with age.[8] Foods high in calcium include dairy products and vegetables, particularly the dark green ones like kale.

Iron deficiency anaemia is also very prevalent amongst older people; the recommended iron intake is 10mg daily, which is equivalent to about four ounces or 100g of meat.

Vitamin C (ascorbic acid) is another very important dietary constituent. Citrus fruits are a major source; it is also found in potatoes and vegetables, but is easily destroyed by overcooking, or the addition of bicarbonate of soda to the cooking water – a technique once very common in this country, to help green vegetables maintain their colour. This vitamin has a vital role to play in the utilisation of other vitamins, and the uptake of iron.

Zinc is also abundantly present in green vegetables; it has a role to play in wound healing, and affects the acuity of taste. Although there are age-related changes in the numbers of taste buds, an adequate amount of dietary zinc can prevent acceleration of the loss of taste.[9]

Fibre is another important dietary consideration for the older person, as it has a vital role in the prevention of constipation – a common problem associated with ageing. The most economical form is raw bran, although if bought from 'health food' shops, it can appear expensive. It can be added to virtually any food, being quite palatable. Certain foods, such as Shredded Wheat (and many less expensive supermarket 'own brands'), are very high in fibre; but perhaps the best sources are fruit and vegetables, as they make up an important part of a balanced diet.

An adequate fluid intake is a vital part of the daily diet; if it is not contraindicated on medical grounds, two litres per day is ideal. It is very important to ensure that fluids are readily accessible to the older person throughout the day.

131

Promoting sound nutrition

Although older people require fewer calories, they are at risk of developing malnutrition for a variety of reasons. They may simply not have enough energy to prepare their own meals; or they might be hampered by alterations in physical mobility and/or vision. It is important to assess their ability to see and taste food, especially if they are to be at home, where they may not notice foodstuffs that have gone bad, should these special senses be impaired.

Additionally, there may be difficulties with shopping. Many older people do not drive, and such small grocery stores that remain in the neighbourhood may be much more expensive than the large supermarkets. Supermarkets themselves can be quite inaccessible in those parts of the country where public transport has become unreliable; and if the person has difficulty managing the large amounts of shopping that may be necessary to offset the cost and trouble of using public transport, the whole effort may not seem worthwhile. For some people, the answer often seems to be 'Meals on Wheels', or to have meals provided in a nearby day centre, should one exist; but these sorts of arrangements do not suit everybody. Some communities have their own shopping and/or transportation services run by the voluntary sector, and these can be much more acceptable to the older person.

The cost of fresh meats, fruits and vegetables may be prohibitive for the older person on a fixed income; and food is frequently packaged in portions or containers that are too large for one or two. Older people, who lived through the depression of the 1930s and the 'austerity years' of the Second World War and beyond, may be reluctant to buy food that might be wasted.

Finally, if the person lives alone there may be no motivation to cook, due to solitude and loneliness. If there is no one with whom meals can be shared, there is a risk of the 'tea and toast' syndrome being established. There are older men who have become widowers, who do not have the first idea about how to prepare a meal, or what constitutes a good diet.

Inadequate nutrition is not confined to older people who live at home. On the acute ward, an older person may be kept starved for a surgical operation or medical investigation that is delayed; in continuing care settings, there may not be enough staff to give the necessary amount of assistance to all the patients or residents who need it. If someone is fed too quickly, and they choke as a result, they are likely to develop a reluctance to eat.

A nutritional assessment must examine both psychosocial and physical parameters. It has been recommended that those who live alone, have a low income, have suffered a recent bereavement, abuse alcohol, or are confused, should be considered as being at high risk for developing malnutrition, and should be referred to a dietitian.[10]

The most nutritionally sound diet in the world is of no use to anyone if it cannot be eaten. Caregivers must pay special attention to the ability of older people to feed themselves, and to chew and swallow foods. Many debilitating conditions, such as stroke or arthritis, may limit self-feeding ability. Caregivers should also give attention to the ability of the person to see their food; it is often helpful to choose plates and dishes of a colour that provides contrast to the food, and to reduce glare. Certain visual conditions, such as glaucoma and cataracts, and the visual changes associated with stroke, may prevent the person from seeing the food at all.

Plates and dishes must be positioned with disabilities in mind. The food should be placed in front of the person, preferably with him or her sitting up to a table that is of the correct height to be able to manipulate cutlery properly. If the person has to be fed, it may be helpful to talk to them during the procedure, telling them what food they are eating. If they are in an upright position, swallowing is made easier, and the normality of dining at a table helps make the procedure seem more natural. The most important thing of all, though, is that the person is given plenty of time.

The condition of the mouth and teeth must be considered carefully; teeth that are in a poor condition, and periodontal disease, will interfere to some extent with the ability to chew and swallow, possibly even making it painful. In this case, it may be necessary to chop or purée food until the problem is resolved.

Ill-fitting dentures can be a major stumbling-block in the effort to get someone to eat an adequate diet; it is essential that a dental referral be made without delay, before other problems arise as a result.

Good oral hygiene must, of course, be maintained; cleaning the mouth and teeth is best done with a toothbrush, and scrupulous attention to the cleanliness of dentures is vital.

Another point worth considering is the person's medication: should medicines be given before, with, or after food? Do any of them leave an aftertaste that might interfere with appetite? Would any of them be taken more easily if given with food? A pharmacist will be able to give advice on this subject.

Guidance for an older person to maintain and promote better nutritional health requires that the caregiver is knowledgeable about nutrition. Cultural, economic and psychosocial factors all have an influence on eating habits; the caregiver must have a good understanding of these factors and the ability to use that information when giving advice to the older person. Knowing when to refer someone on for specialist nutritional counselling, though, is an important part of good nursing practice.

A very comprehensive discussion of all the factors that help or hinder the attainment of good nutrition in the elderly, particularly in the continuing care setting, can be found in an excellent book edited by Denham.[11]

Discussion points

1 Should *all* elderly people who are judged to be 'overweight' be persuaded to go on a reducing diet?
2 If a person you are nursing is diabetic, should sugar be removed from his or her diet?

134

CHAPTER FOURTEEN

The facilitative environment

It is well known that the physical environment influences well-being, learning and functioning. Environment is always a prime concern in schools; desks, chairs, lighting, toilets and other equipment are chosen with a mind to the physical and developmental characteristics of the children who will use them in mind: a young child is not given a chair or desk that was designed for a secondary school pupil. Supplies, such as thick crayons and large print books, are selected to facilitate the learning and development of the children. Similarly, offices are designed with the needs of working adults in mind, so that they can perform at their best; and it should be the same with the continuing care environment, for it is critical to facilitate physical functioning and to achieve the psychosocial well-being of the people for whom these surroundings will be 'home'.

Long-term care facilities

A prime consideration in nursing homes, residential homes (including part III/IV homes) and continuing care wards must be the safety of the residents. Many safety regulations are required by law, set both locally and nationally. Water temperature devices, sanitation rules, electrical systems, handrails, fire alarms, and the minimum amount of space in each person's bed area are just a few examples of these rules. In addition to the legal regulations, there are numerous other safety considerations: call bells must be accessible in all areas, and must be easy to operate; floors must have a non-slip finish or texture and be free of clutter and barriers to mobility; bathrooms, baths and showers must have non-slip mats and/or surfaces, with grab rails installed at the proper levels and so on. The list is a very long one, and periodic inspections of nursing, residential and other homes are carried out to ensure compliance with the law.

It is particularly important to consider the needs of each individual with respect to the environment. For example, if a person has diminished vision or is hemianopic, the positioning of their bed, chair and everything else is of vital importance (see Chapter 8, under 'Cerebrovascular accident', for a discussion of this subject). Beds need to be kept in the low position, except when it is helpful for the person in rising to standing position; bedrails/cotsides may be of use to some people, but they should only be used as safety devices, *never* as restraints; and, of course, the call bell must be accessible at all times.

Chairs and wheelchairs should be properly selected for the older person, with comfortable armrests, seats at the correct height to avoid extreme hip or knee flexion, and backs high enough to support the upper body and head.

While the purpose of wheelchairs is to promote mobility, some have seats which are excessively hard, with implications not just for comfort but also for circulation; and many are not fitted with back- or head supports. If a person is to use a wheelchair, great thought and care must be put into its selection, and whenever possible it must be reserved solely for that individual.

'High-rise' toilet seats, which are easily attached and removed, are of great use to taller people and those with limited hip flexion; these simple and inexpensive items can mean the difference between dependence and independence in using the toilet for many people.

Providing privacy is crucial to the maintenance of a person's well-being; and everyone needs their 'personal space', or own territory. Residents of long-stay facilities tend to establish 'their' areas by frequent use. For example, a bedridden person's personal boundary will be limited to their room (or bedspace, if sharing a room or ward), while someone who is more mobile may quickly establish 'their' chair and place at table. Residents need to be given every opportunity to choose where their effects are to be placed, and their decisions must be respected.

If for any reason a resident has to be moved to another area, careful planning is necessary; and the first thing to establish is that the move is being made for the *person's* benefit, not the *staff's*. The resident should be included in every stage of planning, and encouraged to assist with the packing and repositioning of effects – even if only as the director, if physical participation is not feasible. If the person is to be transferred to another area completely – for example, to an acute ward for investigations – at least one item from the person's environment, such as a favourite picture, should go with them, and its significance explained to the staff at the person's destination. A simple consideration like this can go a long way to lessening relocation confusion.

Caregivers should always knock, or give an audible signal if there is only a curtain, and identify themselves, before entering the person's territory, regardless of that person's physical or cognitive state.

Age-associated decrements in function of the special senses has previously been discussed. With advancing age, increased illumination is needed for general vision and reading, but eyes become more sensitive to glare; therefore, lamp bulbs must be glare-free but sufficiently bright, which means that they have to be chosen carefully. Fluorescent bulbs provide good illumination, but if not properly shaded the glare can be quite intense. In addition, care must be taken, particularly with lamps, to avoid those that generate a lot of heat and could produce burns.

The warm colours (oranges, yellows, reds) are better perceived by older people than the cool colours (blues and greens). It is very helpful to have doorways, hallways and other important places, such as bathrooms, painted in warm colours to aid identification. It may also be helpful to identify a person's room or bed area with their name in letters 2–3 inches high, against a contrasting background, on the door or wall; and if a photograph of the person can be added, this will assist in orientation, as well as helping visitors and staff with identifying that person's area.

While hallways must be kept clear of barriers, there should be chairs or benches should be provided at regular intervals to break up great lengths and provide aesthetic stimulation.

The hearing of older people must also be an environmental consideration. Excessive sound can be very stressful, interfering with rest and possibly leading to disorientation; carpeting, particularly in larger areas such as dining rooms, and hand-held or even earpiece TV/radio sound controls all aid in noise reduction. (For people with hearing aids, induction loops that transmit the TV's sound directly into the aid are essential; and there should be no difficulty in having telephone receivers fitted with similar devices. British Telecom will give advice on this.) Soft chimes or other auditory cues may be used to announce meal times or other events.

An older person's tactile sensation is best stimulated through personal touch. Touching is nurturing, and older people who are touched during conversation respond more positively. However, before doing this, it is important to assess both individual and cultural factors, which may dictate the person's openness to touch. In the environment, this sense can be enhanced through the use of textured wall coverings or hangings, and special fabrics for clothing, and in diversional activities, a variety of materials can be used to augment tactile sensation.

The environment of long-term or continuing care facilities should be used to maximise the person's abilities and comfort, while providing security and privacy. One way of ensuring that these aims are met is to solicit (and act upon) the views of the residents.

Home environment

In the home health care setting, assessment of the environment is crucial to the success of any care plan. If someone is to be discharged from an elderly-care unit in hospital, there is usually an occupational therapist who is highly skilled in this sort of work. There are OTs in some Social Services departments, but they are few and far between; often, the work of assessment falls on the community nursing staff, especially if the person has come from a particularly busy area, such as an acute medical or surgical unit – and then, the assessment takes place *after* discharge.

There are numerous areas that require evaluation, and the process begins at the person's front door; the exterior should be observed for general condition and maintenance. If there are steps, they must be in good repair and have a non-slip surface; spray-on or self-adherent products that provide such a surface can be obtained from hardware or building supply stores. If there are stairs, railings for support must be available and in good repair. Older people often have alterations in their visual perception, so stairways need to be well-lit but glare-free. It is often helpful if the treads of the stairs or steps can be made to contrast with the risers, either by painting, or the application of coloured tape to the riser (not the edge of the tread, as it may work loose and become a hazard). The client must be able to negotiate the stairs or steps safely; this is especially important if there has been a problem with mobility, or there is a current/ potential health problem such as cardiovascular or respiratory disease that may limit activity. If the person is to use a wheelchair, a ramp may be necessary. Although the responsibility for fitting such aids for an older person being discharged from hospital falls on Social Services departments, the increasing pressure of demand in recent years, coupled with budgetary restraints, has led in some areas to extremely long waiting lists; the voluntary sector have taken up some of the workload, but there are vast differences between areas.

The assessor should also observe where the letterbox is located: it should be at an easily accessible height. If it is at the bottom of the door, and the person has difficulty bending, it may need relocating, if possible; if it is higher, a basket can be easily attached to collect the post, obviating the need to pick it up from the floor.

Doors must be easy to open and of adequate width to accommodate assistive devices or wheelchairs. Entrance doors should have locks that are easily operable by the person, whilst being of a good security standard. It is necessary to check that the person knows if anyone is at the door, from wherever they may be in their home, so a doorbell (or flashing light) may have to be installed.

It should also be determined whether or not the person can hear the telephone, and is able to make calls for themselves. Bell amplifiers and signal lights to indicate incoming calls are available from British Telecom. Also, there are push-button telephones available from many stores that have large digital pads, easy to use with arthritic fingers; and there are models with memories, enabling the dialler to use a one- or two-button press for several frequently-used or emergency numbers. Some Social Services departments can also advise on systems such as 'Lifeline', in which the person can wear a pendant that, if pressed in an emergency, however far from the telephone the person might be, an automatic distress call is sent by telephone to one or more predetermined numbers.

If the person does not have a telephone, and either cannot or will not have one installed, a system of summoning help will have to be devised, or a routine of regular checking established with family and/or neighbours.

Smoke alarms should be installed; these have fallen dramatically in price over the past few years, and the few pounds' outlay may be recouped in lower home insurance premiums, now frequently offered to people who have such alarms fitted. The alarm must be clearly audible or visible to the client, and they need to know how to recognise the 'low battery' indicator.

The adequacy of the heating and ventilation systems should be evaluated; the home must be warm enough for the client in winter, and cool enough in periods of hot weather.

The interior of the residence should be evaluated for general cleanliness and safety; the floor should be free of clutter and rugs, particularly if the floor surface is a slippery one. It may be necessary,

139

with the client's permission, to rearrange furniture to create barrier-free pathways. 'Home helps' can usually be arranged through the local Social Services department; there may be a nominal charge, depending on the local authority. Some people prefer to employ someone privately to do light housework, or various voluntary agencies may be able to help out.

Good illumination is essential. Conversion fluorescent light bulbs are relatively inexpensive, easy to install, and helpful in increasing illumination. Extension cords should not be used, unless it is absolutely essential. If they are used they should be run behind furniture and firmly secured to the floor.

The area where food is stored and prepared requires special assessment. Ideally, there should be adequate worktop space, located at the proper height for the client, and the stove should be equipped with controls that the person can easily operate. The local gas and electricity boards will have a person employed to advise on these matters, and adaptations can be arranged speedily through them. Older people should be advised about the risks of wearing loose clothing, such as dressing gowns, when cooking. Pots and pans, dishes and utensils should all be easily accessible. The refrigerator must be capable of maintaining food at the optimum temperature. Some form of refrigeration is essential for most people, particularly if their shopping is done infrequently; if they cannot afford a refrigerator, again, Social Services may be able to help.) The sink should have taps that the client can operate easily.

Unfortunately, many older people do not live in optimal housing, nor do they have adequate financial resources; the person for whom it is recommended that a microwave oven would be ideal may be returning to a single room with a hot-plate positioned precariously on the sideboard. If this is the case, the best that may be possible is minimisation of the risks. All the plugs and cords should be checked, and the use of 'multi-plugs' discouraged. The client may benefit from services such as Meals on Wheels, or a referral to a day centre that provides lunches – but see Chapter 13 for a discussion of the possible drawbacks to these schemes.

The bathroom should be equipped with grab rails located by the bath/shower and toilet. A good idea for some people is that the colour of the toilet seat and sink be made to contrast with the surrounding surfaces; this is easily accomplished with the use of coloured tape or contact paper, though they may need frequent renewal.[1] Special toilet seats are available from medical supply firms. The bath should have a non-slip surface, or have non-slip appliques or strips installed. A sturdy chair or stool may be used for additional safety in the shower. The use of electrical appliances in the bathroom can only be described as a disaster waiting to happen; but if the only available heater for the room is an electric one, then great tact and ingenuity are going to be needed if the person is to be discouraged, and an alternative discovered.

Modifications in sleeping arrangements may have to be made if the client has difficulty in reaching a bedroom that is on a different floor. The assessor should also determine where laundry is done; laundry rooms are frequently located on lower levels of private homes and the same applies in sheltered accommodation and blocks of flats. The client may not have enough mobility or energy to do their own laundry.

Other modifications in the environment may be especially necessary if the person has a chronic brain disorder, such as a dementia of the Alzheimer's type; home care may not be possible at all unless there is a spouse or other person who is willing and able to provide supervision and care. Since people suffering from such disorders tend to wander, it is often helpful to attach 'jingle bells' to exterior doors. It has also been recommended that locks be put near the bottom of the door, where the confused person may not readily find them, and that privacy locks on bathroom doors be altered, allowing them to be opened from the outside. If the person has to be left alone for even the shortest times, however, anything that might prevent their getting out in an emergency needs to be very carefully thought through before it is implemented.[2]

Control knobs of gas stoves may be removed to prevent potential fires or accidental burns; with electric ranges, the master switch can be covered or possibly even moved to a less conspicuous place. Locks should be installed on cupboards that contain hazardous materials, such as cleaning materials or medications; and items of value, such as jewellery and documents, should also be kept in a secure place. Glassware and other breakable objects might have to be kept out of easy reach.

It may be helpful to 'colour-code' the bathroom door in a primary, warm colour using paint or adhesive tape, as an aid to memory. Confused people may have difficulty choosing clothing if they are faced with a great number of items, so it is useful to leave only a few favourite items in wardrobes and drawers to reduce the possibility of this happening.

In the United Kingdom, there are 'hospital loan' or 'community loan' schemes which enable people to borrow, for an indefinite period, equipment such as hospital beds, commodes and so on; community nurses are usually the best informed people about the availability of specific items at any given time. Local authorities, through their Social Services departments, also have stocks of certain items – but this is subject to very wide local variations. The voluntary sector is playing an ever-increasing part in the process of obtaining aids for those who need them, but it is advisable that should any client wish to avail themselves of such a service, the nurse should ensure that the correct aid is chosen with appropriate professional advice.

It is no surprise that the majority of older people want to live in their own homes; as nurses, our duty is to do all we can to make this possible. A thorough assessment of the home environment, coupled with a knowledge of available resources, is an essential component of quality in-home care. The community nurse has a crucial role in ensuring that the person returning to their own home does so with confidence that as many potential problems as possible have been identified and rectified, ensuring that they will be able to stay there for as long as possible.

PART IV

Refining a plan of care

CHAPTER FIFTEEN

Formulation and following up on a plan of care

Introduction

In 1977, the General Nursing Council (which was to be replaced by the UKCC in 1983) decreed that nurses in the United Kingdom would henceforth use something called 'the nursing process'. There was a lot of opposition to this 'new-fangled American nonsense' at first,[1] but through the efforts of the nursing press, those health authorities far-sighted enough to appoint 'nursing process coordinators', and, most importantly of all, the comparatively small number of practising nurses who were open-minded enough to give the idea a try in their areas of work, it eventually became an accepted part of British practice - so much so that it is difficult to believe, now, how much controversy attended its introduction to these shores. If asked, 'What are the stages of the nursing process?', there would not be many nurses in this country who could not reel off 'assessment, planning, implementation and evaluation'. (Note: in this text, the authors use the word 'intervention' instead of 'implementation', a convention which has found favour amongst some nursing writers in this country.)

Yet even as we were struggling with this, nursing theorists in North America were debating whether or not another stage – 'formulating nursing diagnoses'– should be included as a distinct stage in the nursing process, between assessment and planning. Some argued that nursing diagnoses were an integral part of the first stage; others differed. That debate is just about concluded, with the majority of texts agreeing that there are five distinct stages to the process, with nursing diagnosis – a taxonomy for nurses to use in planning care – having established its right to exist, although its exact place in the process will continue to be fought over. 'Whether nursing diagnosis is regarded as a separate component of an artificially divided process may be inconsequential. The important point is that a conscious effort to formulate a nursing diagnosis is made at the conclusion of the nursing process'.[2] That was one nurse's summation in 1991, and it seems to be a reasonable staring point for what follows. (See also the introduction to Part II.)

Nursing plan of care

The foundation of nursing practice lies in the application of the nursing process in day-to-day care. The nursing process is made up of the following components: assessment, diagnosis, planning, intervention and evaluation.[3] The importance of an adequate assessment has been discussed in Chapter 2. Whilst nursing diagnosis is not a new concept, precise taxonomy and language are only now evolving from the National Conferences of Classification of Nursing Diagnosis, first convened in 1973; since 1982, the North American Nursing Diagnosis Association (NANDA) has been constantly at work, refining and streamlining suggestions for inclusion in the classification.

The authors believe that the use of nursing diagnoses is the best way of focusing on the actual or potential health problem(s) of the client. Nursing diagnosis facilitates communication between nurses; discourages 'wastebasket' or inaccurate terminology; facilitates communication between nurses and others; and increases individual accountability.

The problem–etiology–signs/symptoms method of writing nursing diagnoses is espoused by M. Gordon.[4] This format suggests a problem statement in concise terms that leads to identification of nursing goals and nursing interventions. The format is useful because the nursing interventions are determined easily by stating the aetiology of the health problem. The statement of the aetiology must be amenable to nursing practice. Examples of nursing diagnoses, goals and interventions for various health problems have been described in Part II of this book.

The key to effective delivery of nursing services is a *written* plan of care that reflects the health problems and needs of the older person. The plan of care is based on data obtained through accurate assessment. of The client's participation is imperative for planning and providing quality care. Nurses in the United States have established standards of gerontological practice by which to measure the quality of nursing care. Thus the nurse is responsible and accountable to the recipient of his or her services. It is essential that the nurse has knowledge of the standards in order to achieve high quality practice. The standards of gerontological nursing practice are given in Appendix A towards the end of this book.

The plan of care is individualised, specific, *goal-orientated* and derived from the nursing diagnoses. A goal is the eventual outcome of a health problem that the nurse and the patient/client hope to attain. Short-term goals are usually those that may be achieved within a brief period. Long term goals are those statements of the desired results of the nursing care. The formulation of these goals serves as the basis for discharge planning and evaluation of nursing care.[5]

Evaluation and quality assurance

Evaluation and quality assurance of nursing care reflect the completion or lack of completion of the nursing process. Were the nursing interventions successful, and were the goals achieved?

Evaluation

Evaluation is the component of the nursing process that judges the validity of the nursing diagnoses and effectiveness of the nursing interventions. Evaluation may lead to a decision that the assessment, nursing diagnoses and subsequent interventions were accurate and appropriate. On the other hand, evaluation may lead to the conclusion that the assessment, diagnoses, or interventions were *inaccurate*, and that revision is required.

An example of an evaluation resulting in the decision of accuracy of nursing diagnosis is the following:

After establishment of the nursing diagnosis of potential impairment of skin integrity due to immobility/bedrest, nursing interventions ordered included skin cleansing/lubrication protocols, and repositioning schedules. These interventions were documented in the resident's chart (nursing notes). The resident did not develop any pressure sores; hence, the nursing diagnosis and interventions were accurate and valid.

An example of an evaluation resulting in a decision that the assessment and interventions were inaccurate is the following:

A nursing diagnosis of impaired verbal communication due to cerebrovascular accident was established for a person who spoke only unintelligible phrases after a CVA. Nursing interventions included

147

directions for speaking to the person as well as orders for the use of an assistive communication device. The goal was establishment and maintenance of communication. After one week it was noted that the person continued to use only 'garbled' phrases. A careful review of the history revealed that the person did not speak English, but a mid-European language. This was verified after arranging for a visit by a person conversant in this specific language.

Although the diagnosis of impaired verbal communication was accurate, the aetiology was inaccurate. The person was able to communicate, but not in English. The nursing staff and interpreter devised a 'word list' for use in communicating with the person. The original list of nursing interventions was changed. Communication with the person was finally achieved.

An example of an evaluation which resulted in the decision that the assessment, nursing diagnosis and interventions were inaccurate is the following: The nursing diagnosis of sleep pattern disturbance due to stress was formulated when it was observed that an older patient constantly awoke at 4.00 a.m. and was fatigued by 1.00 p.m. The afternoon fatigue interfered with his physiotherapy. Nursing interventions included the administration of the prescribed (prn) hypnotic, the patient's favourite warm beverage at bedtime, and environment quieting measures. However, the patient continued to awaken early and his lethargy increased.

A review of recent literature[6] and a review of the patient's sleep history led to the conclusion that the pattern of early awakening and the need for an afternoon nap were normal for the patient. It was postulated that the hypnotic influenced the increased lethargy. The diagnosis of 'decreased activity tolerance due to fatigue' was formulated. The physiotherapy session was rescheduled for later in the afternoon; the patient completed his bath and other morning activities when he awakened at 4.00 a.m. The prn hypnotic was omitted; the warm beverage continued being offered. The patient was subsequently able to participate without fatigue in his therapy and was no longer lethargic.

Evaluation is also an important component of that activity known as quality assurance (QA), a subject that is growing in importance in Britain all the time; many health authorities have appointed nurses to work exclusively with QA. As audits of care become routine – as they undoubtedly will during the next few years – no nurse will be untouched by some form of QA in her daily practice.

A concise diagnostic statement defines the outcome desired for evaluation, audit and QA activities; hence, the the use of nursing diagnosis also simplifies the process of evaluation.[7]

Quality assurance

One way of defining this rather nebulous term is as that activity which assures the consumer of a specified degree of excellence through continuous measurement and evaluation of structural components, goal-directed nursing process and/or consumer outcome. Pre-established criteria, standards and available norms are used in the activity.[8]

The most important component of QA is compliance with standards of gerontological practice. Through evaluation it can be determined if:

1 Data have been collected and recorded.
2 Nursing diagnoses have been formulated.
3 A workable plan of care and goals have been developed from the nursing diagnoses.
4 Interventions amenable to nursing practice have been identified and prioritised.
5 The nursing care has been delivered.
6 Collaboration between the client and the nurse has been achieved in the planning and provision of nursing care.

Nurses should welcome the opportunity to serve on QA committees. The importance of evaluation of total care is an integral function of all health care disciplines. (The interested reader is referred to suggested nursing care plans in the case studies presented in the next chapter.)

Multidisciplinary plan of care

The only effective way to plan care is by taking a multi- (or, as some would prefer) inter-disciplinary approach.[9] Although the degree of democracy within teams can vary considerably,[10] there is no doubt that different disciplines can pull in opposite directions, if left uncoordinated; some readers will have experienced this at first hand, on those occasions when communication, for whatever reason, has suffered a temporary breakdown.

The disciplines include (but are not limited to) nursing, medicine, administration, social services, rehabilitative services, and nutrition. The purposes of utilising this approach are to involve the person in planning his or her care, to delineate clearly goals and responsibilities of each care provider, and to avoid redundancies or omissions

149

in the provision of care. The multidisciplinary approach to care planning and provision begins with the initial interview and assessment, which has been described in Chapter 1.

It is most important that the *nursing* plan of care be developed before the multi disciplinary planning conference. By virtue of 24-hour contact with the person, nursing has the most information about the actual and potential needs of the person, and therefore can serve as a guide to other members in care planning. Collaboration with the multi disciplinary team may result in modifications in the nursing plan of care.

Considerations in home health (community) care

Community care is the most rapidly expanding field of nursing practice, and most home care patients are elderly. Each home care situation is unique and requires complex and multi faceted care. Clients who receive community care may be discharged home following surgery or an illness, a newly-diagnosed or chronic health problem, or a terminal illness. Another type of client may be the older person who needs assistance to remain in his or her home. In these nursing situations, the nurse focuses on the prevention of problems and maximisation the client's function. There have been several initiatives in Britain designed to enable older people to remain in their own homes, the most recent being the government white paper, *Care in the Community* (London: HMSO, 1991) as the central legislature realise that it is a much more cost-efficient alternative to institutional care.

The community nurse does not always have the advantages of the hospital-based practitioner, who has direct access to members of the multidisciplinary team, and exercises a great deal of control over the person's environment, but the goals remain the same for both: helping the client maintain independence, whilst reaching his or her health potential.

During the initial visit to an individual's home, a biographical database is begun, to obtain health data. Communication techniques are necessary to establish a relationship of trust with the client. The nurse must ask permission to enter the person's home, unlike the situation in an institutional setting. The client must be assured that all information is confidential. The nurse should relate the purpose of the visit at the outset, and indicate the amount of time the interview is expected to take. Having identified who the nurse is and by what name the client prefers to be called, the nurse is then able to begin a total health assessment. Observational skills are most important during this assessment, as they are throughout the whole home visit.

It is recommended that the nurse uses an assessment instrument to assist in collecting data. The same subjective assessment worksheet that was provided in Chapter 1 may be used in the home situation. The nurse should, however, choose tools that meet the needs of her particular clients.

Assessment of objective data, or the physical examination, begins when the nurse meets the client. The physical assessment worksheet that was given in Chapter 2 is one example of a tool that the nurse may use as a guide through the physical examination, which then completes the total health database.

Following the comprehensive nursing assessment, the nurse should analyse the data gathered, reach a conclusion about the client's health status, and formulate the nursing diagnoses. Nursing interventions can be developed using the equipment and supplies that the client is familiar with, and with which the nurse may improvise.

The nurse must carefully assess the abilities of the client and the principle caregiver(s) to determine if the most appropriate level of care can be administered in the home. The nurse also serves as an advocate for the client and his or her family. Since the focus of medical practice is often on the management of acute illness, it is not uncommon for a GP to suggest hospital or some other form of institutional care, without a thorough assessment of the client's capabilities or support systems. It can be the nurse's role to help keep older people in their familiar home environment.

A thorough assessment by the nurse can help determine if the client has adequate capability and support to remain at home. During hospitalisation for an acute illness, both the client and the family may be overwhelmed by the amount of supplies and technical expertise required for care and believe that care in the home is not possible. However, it is not always necessary to use expensive or disposable equipment in the home environment. For example, urinary catheters for intermittent catheterisation may be safely cleaned with soap and water and stored in a plastic bag in the home. Similarly, oxygen cannulae and certain suction equipment need not be disposed of after each use or within a given time frame. Also, procedures that may appear to be highly technical, such as intravenous infusions, can be taught to the client and/or their caregivers at home through one-to-one education and provision of proper resources.

The nurse must assess and respect the wishes of the client and the family. In some cases, clients may not want to be nursed at home, or have the necessary resources for a nursing home. It has been the experience of the authors that significant numbers of older people do not regard nursing homes negatively, and have, in fact, planned over the years for such long-term care. The authors feel that this belief is due principally to a client's desire not to burden the spouse and family; moreover, this belief may have been mutually agreed upon by the client, spouse and family members. Also, the authors believe that positive attitudes towards nursing homes often evolve when the client has friends in long-term care facilities, or when the person has had positive experiences with long-term care. The function of the nurse may be to determine if the client is a candidate for home health care, or if an alternative level of care is more congruent with client needs, abilities and wishes.

In the United States, S. Hewner defined the role of home care nurses by asking: 'What is the most important thing you do to help this person stay at home?' From their answers, Hewner developed twelve empirical groups of nursing interventions; of these, monitoring health status, health teaching, and caregiver support were the categories that nurses used most frequently.[11] The authors believe that the major role of the community nurse is the rapport that exists between the nurse, the family, and the client. Adaptation of the home environment, education of the caregiver and client, and frequent evaluation of the client's abilities, are some of the unique array of services given to older people. The support and companionship offered by the nurse is the key to success in maintaining clients in their own homes.

Discussion points

1 Is home *always* the best place for someone to be nursed?
2 If someone is adamant that they wish to be cared for at home, but you feel that there could be a disaster as a result, to what lengths would you go to keep that person in hospital?

CHAPTER SIXTEEN

Selected case studies

The following five case studies are designed to demonstrate implementation of the nursing process with older clients receiving nursing care in acute, continuing care, and community settings. The case studies are organised as in previous chapters using the format of nursing diagnosis and nursing interventions. Examples of goals and discussion of evaluations are also included.

Case study A

Mrs Joyce Smith, a 91-year-old widow who lives alone in the small village of Moresby, is admitted to the ward from accident and emergency (A & E). She is known to be diabetic, controlled on insulin. She was brought to A & E by a neighbour, who said that Mrs Smith had complained of feeling dizzy, and seemed to be very confused.

Blood glucose on admission was 48 mmol/litre (normal range, 3.5–6.5). Urinalysis showed glycosuria, more than 2 per cent, but no ketonuria. Sliding scale insulin and intravenous fluids have been started in A & E.

Nursing diagnosis no. 1

Alteration in fluid volume, actual, related to inadequate hydration resulting in dry skin and mucous membranes, decreased skin turgor, confusion.

Short-term goal: resolution of altered metabolic state.
Long-term goal: adequate diabetic control at home.

Nursing interventions

1 Monitor blood glucose levels every four hours with re-agent strips (for example BM sticks, Dextrostrips).
2 Administer insulin as per sliding scale instructions.
3 Observe for rapid onset of hypoglycaemia as blood glucose level falls.
4 Assess skin for turgor, and mucous membranes for dryness.
5 Monitor intravenous fluids.
6 Measure intake and output hourly.

Nursing diagnosis no. 2

Potential for injury due to confusion and vertigo.

Nursing interventions

1 Maintain safety precautions.
2 Do not restrain.
3 Implement reality orientation measures.
4 Record level of consciousness/orientation hourly.

Nursing diagnosis no. 3

Knowledge deficit of management of diabetes.

Nursing interventions

1 Implement diabetic teaching plan.
2 Arrange for dietitian to visit Mrs Smith.
3 Arrange for community nurse to visit after discharge.
4 Contact Social Services, via liaison social worker, for advice on feasibility of special meals being provided by either the home care team, Meals on Wheels, the local day centre, or any other alternatives.

Evaluation

1 Blood sugar maintained at safe level.
2 Adequate hydration achieved by measuring intake and output, skin turgor.
3 Orientated to time, place and person.
4 Diabetic teaching plan implemented and evaluated.
5 Community nurse, dietitian and Social Services contacted, and they will discuss arrangements for home care with Mrs Smith.

154

Short-term goal is achieved and long-term goal is in the process of being achieved.

Case study B

Mrs Doris Gooding, an 87-year-old widow, is transferred to a slow-stream rehabilitation ward eight days after having had a Thompson's hemiarthroplasty, after a fracturing the neck of her left femur. Physiotherapy was begun on the orthopaedic ward, but progress is slow due to residual effects of a previous CVA. Activity is limited to transfer from bed to chair for 30 minutes a day. She has an indwelling catheter.

Nursing diagnosis no. 1

Impaired physical mobility related to restriction of movement, resulting in inability to walk.
Short-term goal: urinary continence following catheter removal.
Long-term goal: ambulation – Mrs Gooding will walk with assistive device.

Nursing interventions

1   Arrange physiotherapy assessment.
2   Speak to the nurse who was Mrs Gooding's principal carer (primary nurse, team leader) on the orthopaedic ward.
3   Arrange multi-disciplinary meeting at the first opportunity.
4   Instruct Mrs Gooding in range of movement (ROM) exercises, which she is to perform three times a day.
5   Sit her up in a suitable chair for meals.

Nursing diagnosis no. 2

Potential for impairment of skin integrity due to immobility.

Nursing interventions

1   Place pressure-relieving mattress on bed, and suitable cushion on chair.
2   Ensure that pressure is relieved by change of position at least two-hourly (include standing).
3   Assess pressure areas when position is changed.

Nursing diagnosis no. 3

Potential for urinary infection associated with indwelling catheter.

Nursing interventions

1 Observe strict asepsis if catheter has to be handled.
2 Offer at least 200ml of fluid every two hours.
3 Maintain closed drainage system.
4 Remove catheter at the first opportunity.

Evaluation

1 Multi disciplinary conference held and ambulation begun.
2 Joint mobility maintained.
3 Skin integrity maintained.
4 Urinary catheter removed with no evidence of infection present.

Case study C

Mr John Beaumont is an 83-year-old widower, who ran his own farm up to the age of seventy. He has just been admitted as a resident in a nursing home. His medical diagnosis is arteriosclerotic and cerebral vascular disease. A CAT scan showed cortical atrophy. He is disoriented to person, time and place. Recently he has refused foods or fluids by spitting out anything given to him. It is thought that he has a dementia of the Alzheimer type.

Nursing diagnosis no. 1

Alteration in nutrition, less than body requirements due to inability to eat/drink, resulting in dry skin and mucous membranes, decreased skin turgor.
Short-term goal: increase oral intake to 2000ml/day.
Long-term goal: prevention of injuries and maintenance of safety measures.

Nursing interventions

1 Maintain accurate records of intake.
2 Attempt 2-week trial of feeding in his room.

156

3 Prior to mealtime:
   (a) Lightly stroke around the mouth three times with an ice cube.
   (b) Stroke three times from ear lobe to corner of mouth with ice cube.
   (c) Stroke three times along jawbone to centre of chin with ice cube.
4 Mealtime:
   (a) Give no puréed foods – only chewables.
   (b) Present one food at a time.
   (c) Use straws with all liquids.
5 Weigh weekly, at the same time of day, using the same scales.

Nursing diagnosis no. 2

Memory deficit related to perceptive/cognitive impairment resulting in disorientation

Nursing interventions

1 Assess and record level of orientation weekly by using MSQ tests.
2 Use name sign on bed.
3 Reminiscence therapy every afternoon:
   (a) Discuss past farming activities.
   (b) Discuss Mrs Beaumont's role in running their farm.

Nursing diagnosis no. 3

Potential for physical injury due to impaired judgement

Nursing interventions

1 Tape over privacy locks.
2 Keep bells that jingle on his door.
3 Mr Beaumont is to wear an identity bracelet with his name and address written clearly on it.
4 Safety measures implemented:
   (a) Bed in low position.
   (b) All breakable and thus potentially harmful objects removed from his room.

Evaluation

1 Oral intake of 2000ml/day achieved.
2 He has maintained admission weight.
3 No physical injuries to date.
4 Level of orientation has not worsened since admission.

Case study D

Mr Iain McPherson, a 93-year-old bachelor, is transferred to a continuing care ward from the acute elderly medical unit. He is fully aware of his medical diagnoses, which include malignant lymphoma and a compromised nutritional status. Before he was transferred, he asked to see the consultant, to make it plain that he did not want to receive any aggressive medical treatment; the consultant agreed, and entered in the medical notes: 'For comfort measures only'. Mr McPherson has a large sacral pressure sore. He cannot feed himself, is very weak, but is fully orientated to time, place and person. He has only distant nieces and nephews. Whilst in the acute ward, he constantly expressed a wish to die, and has continued to feel this way since transfer. He has intermittent pain, which responds well to diamorphine, 5mg subcutaneously.

Nursing diagnosis no. 1

Depleted health potential associated with knowledge of terminal disease process and knowledge of impending death, resulting in verbalisation of death wish, and generalised pain.
Short-term goals:

1 Relief of pain.
2 Effective nursing management of pressure sore.
3 Maintenance of hydration.

Long-term goal: Mr McPherson will be able to verbalise acceptance of impending death and participate in final plans (for example, funeral arrangements, distribution of his estate).

Nursing interventions

1 Explore with him his statements about wanting to die.
2 Determine how long he thinks he is going to live.
3 Investigate support systems (for example, contact his nieces and nephews, with his permission, identify potential friends).

158

4 Assess spiritual needs – identify clergyman of choice if appropriate.
5 Assess cultural expectations of the dying process (for example funeral arrangements).
6 Determine whether Mr McPherson has made appropriate legal arrangements.
7 Investigate the possibility of a referral to the hospice symptom control team.

Nursing diagnosis no. 2

Alteration in comfort: pain related to knowledge deficit of pain management technique resulting in verbalisations of pain.

Nursing interventions

1 Assess scope of pain (for example on a scale of 1 to 10).
2 In conjunction with medical and pharmacy staff, titrate analgesia dosage.
3 Investigate other methods of pain relief (for example therapeutic touch, massage, transcutaneous electrical nerve stimulation – TENS).

Nursing diagnosis no. 3

Impairment of skin integrity; actual due to open sore on sacrum, 2.5cm diameter

Nursing interventions

1 Assess pressure areas and record status at regular intervals.
2 Sacral sore:
   (a) Clean with normal saline.
   (b) Apply hydrocolloid dressing.
   (c) Change as necessary.
3 Use a pressure-relieving mattress.
4 Ensure pressure relief through positional changing, at least two hourly, or to Mr McPherson's tolerance.

Nursing diagnosis no. 4

Alteration in nutrition, less than body requirements, related to inability to eat and drink; resulting in loss of weight, loss of appetite, pale conjunctiva, and dry mucous membranes.

Nursing interventions

1 Record daily intake and output.
2 Refer to dietitian for advice.
3 Determine and provide food of Mr McPherson's choice, wherever possible.

Evaluation

He is pain-free without clouding of sensorium. The wound's healing has not progressed, but it has not worsened. Contacts have been made with members of a potential support system. Funeral arrangements are in hand.

Case study E

Tommy Jackson is a 69-year-old man who lives in a warden-controlled flat owned by a charitably-run housing association; he and his wife moved there four years ago, after he retired from his job as a motor mechanic. Their GP recommended the move, as Mr Jackson has chronic bronchitis, and it seemed advisable that he should be somewhere where help was at hand, should he fall ill. His wife, too, suffers from chronic ill-health; two years ago she had a CVA and fractured the neck of her femur in the fall. Since then, she has been in a private nursing home. They have no children. Mr Jackson goes to see his wife on alternate Sundays which involves travelling on two buses. He developed a gastric ulcer about a year ago, and it gives him occasional trouble.

He feels that the flat is adequate for his needs; there are smoke alarms, and the bathroom has safety bars and non-slip mats. The warden checks that he is all right every morning, via the intercom, and he visits the couple in the flat next door every day. He has a telephone.

He eats one meal a day at a local volunteer-run day centre, and has a home help once a week. He receives only the basic old age pension; as they had no savings, the cost of his wife's nursing home care is currently met by the state. He has been referred to the community nursing service by the geriatrician who diagnosed his ulcer, and who sees him in Outpatients every six months.

Mr Jackson says that his health is 'not good'. His main problem is 'getting enough air', and he describes a history of 'blacking out' after 'coughing fits', and 'shakiness' of his right arm, which causes him to have problems preparing meals. His legs ache if he walks more than a couple of hundred yards. He wishes that he could give up smoking.

Current medications include: salbutamol inhaler, two puffs four times a day; ranitidine, 300mg daily; and temazepam, 20mg at night. He formerly took an unknown steroid drug for his pulmonary condition. He smokes forty untipped cigarettes a day, does not drink alcohol, and has two cups of caffeinated coffee in the morning.

He reports some deficit in hearing, and wears bifocal glasses; both hearing and vision were checked at his last Outpatient's appointment. He also states that food 'doesn't smell or taste as good as it used to', which he partially attributes to the large-volume cooking done at the day centre.

He seems somewhat anxious, but he is otherwise alert and well orientated. Recent and remote memory are intact. He usually wakes up around 7 a.m., 'but it takes me a bit to get going', because of excessive coughing and sputum production; coughing also causes him to waken several times during the night. He usually eats bran flakes with milk, two rounds of toast, and two cups of coffee for breakfast; the day centre provides a meal of meat and two vegetables, bread and butter, milk and a pudding at lunchtimes; supper is usually a sandwich, tinned milk pudding, and a glass of milk. It is difficult for him to chew, because he only has two teeth. Mr Jackson says that his appetite 'used to be better', and the occasional upper abdominal pain that occurs is blamed on his ulcer.

He says that he has no problems with urinary incontinence. He is often bothered with constipation, passing a hard, brown stool every other day. The normal time of defaecation is after breakfast; it involves much straining, and usually leaves him breathless.

He has no leisure activities or hobbies. He often sleeps in his chair and always uses two pillows when he sleeps in bed. He can meet his own hygiene needs independently. He tries to conserve his energies for visiting his wife.

He has shortness of breath, which limits his activity, and coughs with copious sputum. Hot, humid weather increases his dyspnoea. Although the flat has central heating, he does not have a humidifier.

Mr Jackson wishes that his health was better. He also wishes that he could take care of his wife, or at least have enough energy to visit her more frequently. He has many financial concerns, and is worried that if the nursing home increases its charges, he will have to make up the difference out of his own pocket between what the state will pay and the new level. He is lonely most of the time, but does not

161

have enough energy for any more social contacts than he already has.

Nursing diagnosis no. 1

Ineffective airway clearance related to thoracic breathing and chronic smoking.
Short-term goal: practice breathing exercises.
Long-term goals:

1   refer to 'stop smoking' clinic.
2   Increase activity and socialisation.

Nursing interventions

1   Provide a developmental environment for learning (that is good lighting, quiet, privacy).
2   Explain the pathogenesis of emphysema in lay terminology.
3   Demonstrate pursed lip breathing exercises:
    (a)   Assume a comfortable, upright position.
    (b)   Inhale through the nose.
    (c)   Hold breath momentarily.
    (d)   Exhale through pursed lips in a whistling position.
4   Provide and explain monitoring tool (checklist) of number of times exercises are performed.
5   Find a way of humidifying the air (for example, putting shallow dishes of water on the radiators, or boiling water on the stove).
6   Refer to 'stop smoking' programme or clinic.

Nursing diagnosis no. 2

Potential for fluid volume deficit associated with knowledge deficiency related to fluid intake.

Nursing interventions

1   Instruct on the need for 6–8 glasses of fluid daily.
2   Determine his fluid preferences (include milk puddings).
3   Ask him to record his fluid intake.
4   Teach the complications associated with fluid volume deficit:
    (a)   Metabolic imbalance.
    (b)   Dry skin.
    (c)   Dry bronchial secretions.
    (d)   Excessive fatigue related to coughing dry secretions.

162

Nursing diagnosis no. 3

Alteration in nutrition, less than body requirements, related to inability to obtain and prepare food, poor dentition, anorexia.

Nursing interventions

1 Refer Mr Jackson to dental services.
2 Liaise with Social Services, to see if home help can be increased to include some shopping.
3 Provide at least one more meal daily, through Meals on Wheels.
4 Develop a list of food preferences.

Nursing diagnosis no. 4

Sleep pattern disturbance related to coughing episodes, impaired oxygen transport, and lack of exercise.

Nursing interventions

1 Obtain a history of sleep pattern and sleep rituals.
2 Ask the GP to prescribe a simple linctus that can be kept at the bedside.
3 Instruct Mr Jackson in relaxation techniques.

Nursing diagnosis no. 5

Grieving, dysfunctional, related to impairment of health status of self and wife, and unavailable social support system.

Nursing interventions

1 Positive reinforcement of positive aspects of health status (successes in attaining health goals).
2 Encourage him to telephone his wife daily, and check the availability of volunteer transport services in the area.

Nursing diagnosis no. 6

Potential for injury (trauma) due to falls.

Nursing interventions

1 Eliminate unsafe rugs.

2 Create a barrier-free environment; discuss with Mr Jackson the ways in which his furniture could be arranged to make the flat safer for him.

Nursing diagnosis no. 7

Alteration in elimination; constipation related to lack of exercise and decreased fluid intake.

Nursing interventions

1 Suggest intake of whole fruit juices.
2 Instruct sedentary exercises on a daily routine.
3 Increase fluid intake to 6–8 glasses daily.
4 Encourage same-time elimination pattern.

Evaluation

Mr Jackson has become less short of breath and has enrolled in a 'stop smoking' programme, though he has yet to attend his first class. Meals on Wheels are providing one extra meal a day. His home help has had her hours increased, so that she can do a little more regular shopping for him. He says that he is more rested on awakening. Cough medicine is only needed once a night. He is visiting Mrs Jackson three times a week, with the help of the volunteer driver service. He has not had any falls, and the constipation problem is resolved.

American Nurses' Association Standards of Gerontological Nursing Practice*

Standard I

Data collected about the health status of the older adult are systematically and continuously. The data are accessible, communicated and recorded.

Standard II

Nursing diagnoses are derived from the identified normal responses of the individual to ageing and the data collected about the health status of the older adult.

Standard III

A plan of nursing care is developed in conjunction with the older adult and/or significant others, that includes goals derived from the nursing diagnosis.

Standard IV

The plan of nursing care includes priorities and prescribed nursing approaches, and measures to achieve the goals derived from the nursing diagnosis.

* American Nurses' Association. 1976. *Standards of Gerontological Nursing Practice*. Kansas City, MO: American Nurses' Association.

Standard V

The plan of care is implemented, using appropriate nursing actions.

Standard VI

The older adult and/or significant other(s) participate in determining the process attained in the achievement of established goals.

Standard VII

The older adult and/or significant others participate in the ongoing process of assessment, the setting of new goals, the reordering of priorities, the revision of plans for nursing care, and the initiation of new nursing actions.

Approved nursing diagnoses (North American Nursing Diagnosis Association–NANDA) 1990

Activity intolerance
Activity intolerance, potential
Adjustment, impaired
Airway clearance, ineffective
Altered nutrition: more than body requirements
Altered nutrition: less than body requirements
Altered nutrition: potential for more than body requirements
Altered protection
Anxiety
Aspiration, potential for
Body image disturbance
Body temperature, altered: potential
Bowel incontinence
Breast feeding, effective
Breast feeding, ineffective
Breathing pattern, ineffective
Cardiac output, decreased
Communication, impaired: verbal
Constipation
Constipation, colonic
Constipation, perceived
Coping, defensive
Coping, family: potential for growth
Coping, ineffective family: compromised
Coping, ineffective family: disabling
Coping, ineffective individual
Decisional conflict (specify)

Denial, ineffective
Diarrhoea
Disuse syndrome, potential for
Diversional activity deficit
Dysreflexia
Family processes, altered
Fatigue
Fear
Fluid volume deficit
Fluid volume deficit, potential
Fluid volume excess
Gas exchange, impaired
Grieving, anticipatory
Grieving, dysfunctional
Growth and development, altered
Health maintenance, altered
Health-seeking behaviours (specify)
Home maintenance management, impaired
Hopelessness
Hyperthermia
Hypothermia
Infection, potential for
Injury, potential for
Knowledge deficit (specify)
Mobility, impaired physical
Noncompliance (specify)
Oral mucous membrane, altered
Pain
Pain, chronic
Parental role conflict
Parenting, altered
Parenting, altered: potential
Personal identity disturbance
Poisoning, potential for
Post-trauma response
Powerlessness
Rape-trauma syndrome
Rape-trauma syndrome: compound reaction
Rape-trauma syndrome: silent reaction
Role-performance, altered
Self-care deficit: bathing/hygiene
Self-care deficit: dressing/grooming

Self-care deficit: feeding
Self-care deficit: toileting
Self-esteem disturbance
Self-esteem, low: chronic
Self-esteem, low: situational
Sensory-perceptual alterations: visual, auditory, kinaesthetic, gustatory, tactile, auditory (specify)
Sexual dysfunction
Sexuality, altered patterns
Skin integrity, impaired
Skin integrity, impaired: potential
Sleep pattern disturbance
Social interaction, impaired
Social isolation
Spiritual distress (distress of the human spirit)
Suffocation, potential for
Swallowing, impaired
Thermoregulation, impaired
Thought processes, altered
Tissue integrity, impaired
Tissue perfusion, altered: renal, cerebral, cardiopulmonary, gastro-intestinal, peripheral (specify type)
Trauma, potential for
Unilateral neglect
Urinary elimination, altered
Urinary incontinence, functional
Urinary incontinence, reflex
Urinary incontinence, stress
Urinary incontinence, total
Urinary incontinence, urge
Urinary retention
Violence, potential for: self-directed or directed at others

Introduction

1 Bury, M. and Holme, A. 1991. *Life after Ninety*. London: Routledge, 1.
2 Coni, N., Davison, W. and Webster, S. 1988. *Lecture Notes on Geriatrics* (3rd edn). Oxford: Blackwell Scientific Publications, 19.
3 *Guardian*, 8 May 1991 (Society Today).
4 *Project 2000: A new Preparation for Practice*. 1986. London: UKCC.

Chapter 1

1 For a discussion of various classifications of ADLs, see Twining, C. 1991. Quality of Life: Assessment and Improvement. In Denham, M. J. (ed.), *Care of the Long-Stay Elderly Patient* (2nd edn). London: Chapman and Hall.
2 Sendell, B. and Hunt, P. 1987. *Nursing the Adult with a Specific Physiological Disturbance* (2nd edn). London: Macmillan.
3 Booth, B. 1990. Does it really matter at that age? *Nursing Times* **86**(3), 50–2.

Chapter 2

1 Morton, P. G. (ed.) 1990. *Health Assessment (Nurse's Clinical Guide)*. Springhouse, Pa.: Springhouse Corporation.
2 Eliopoulos, C. 1984. *Health Assessment of the Older Adult*. Reading, Mass.: Addison-Wesley.
3 Coni, N., Davison, W. and Webster, S. 1988. *Lecture Notes on Geriatrics* (3rd edn). Oxford: Blackwell Scientific Publications, 19.
4 Storer, R. 1985. The gastrointestinal system – the oral tissues. In Brocklehurst, J. C. (ed.) 1985. *Textbook of Geriatric Medicine and Gerontology* (3rd edn). Edinburgh: Churchill Livingstone.
5 Thurlbeck, W. M. 1981. The ageing lung. In Scadding, J. G. and Cumming, G. (eds), *Scientific Foundations of Respiratory Medicine*. London: Heinemann.
6 Armstrong, M. and Cleary, M. 1982. *Physiology of Ageing, Part II*. Villanova, Pa.: ProScientia.
7 Interpreting arterial blood gases. 1980. *American Journal of Nursing* **80** (12), 2197–2201.

8   Carotenuto, R. and Bullock, J. 1980. *Physical Assessment of Gerontological Client*. Philadelphia, Pa.: Davis.
9   Malasanos, L., Barkauskas, V., Moss M. and Stoltenberg-Allen, K. 1981. *Health Assessment*. St. Louis, Miss.: Mosby.
10 Walsh, M. and Ford, P. 1989. *Nursing Rituals: Research and Rational Actions*. Oxford: Heinemann Nursing.
11 Caird, F. I., Dall, J. L. C. and Williams, B. O. 1985. The cardiovascular system. In Brocklehurst, J. C. (ed.), *Textbook of Geriatric Medicine*.
12 Matteson, M. A. and McConnell, E. S. (eds) 1988. *Gerontological Nursing: Concepts and Practice*. Philadelphia, Pa.: W. B. Saunders.
13 Dayan, A. D. and Lewis, P. D. 1985. The central nervous system – neuropathology of ageing. In Brocklehurst, J. C. (ed.), *Textbook of Geriatric Medicine*.
14 Alcott, D. 1990. Normal ageing. In Stokes, G. and Goudie, F., *Working with Dementia*. Bicester, Oxon.: Winslow Press.
15 An excellent text, which covers the subject of memory and the older person comprehensively, is by Twining, C. 1991. *The Memory Handbook*. Bicester, Oxon.: Winslow Press.
16 Estimates vary between texts, from definite percentages to general statements, hedged with qualifications. For example, in Martin, A. and Gambrill, E. C. 1986. Geriatrics. Lancaster: MTP Press, the authors state that 'psychiatric disorders' in the over-65s is 'around 5%', rising to 'over 20%' by age 80; but Post reviews a large number of surveys, without giving any definitive estimates, in Post, F. 1985. The central nervous system – the emotional disorders. In Brocklehurst J. C. (ed.) *Textbook of Geriatric Medicine*.
17 Malasanos *et al.* 1981. *Health Assessment*.
18 Goudie, F. 1990. Intellectual and behavioural assessment. In Stokes, G. and Goudie, F. *Working with Dementia*.
19 Pathy, M. S. J. 1985. The central nervous system – clinical presentation and management of neurological disorders in old age. In Brocklehurst, J. C. (ed.).
20 Ibid.
21 Blacklock, N. J. 1985. The genitourinary system – the prostate. In Brocklehurst, J. C. (ed.) *Textbook of Geriatric Medicine*.
22 In the editor's opinion, the best book on this subject to have been published to date is by Gibson, H. B. 1992. *The Emotional and Sexual Lives of Older People – A Manual for Professionals*. London: Chapman and Hall.
23 Bellack, J. and Bamford, P. 1984. *Nursing Assessment: A Multi-dimensional Approach*. Monterey, Calif.: Wadsworth Health Science Division.
24 Sundwall, D., Rolando, J. and Thorne, G. 1981. Endocrine and metabolic function. In O'Hara-Devereaux, M., Andrus, L. and Scott, C. (eds) 1981. *Eldercare*. New York: Grune and Stratton.
25 For a comprehensive discussion of theories of ageing, see ch. 5 of Matteston, M. A. and McConnell, E. S. 1988. *Gerontological Nursing*.
26 Davies, I. 1985. Biology of ageing – general principles. In Brocklehurst, J. C. *Textbook of Geriatric Medicine*.

Part II Introduction

1 *Nursing Times* commissioned two articles in 1992 about the possible use of nursing diagnoses in this country: one for, and one against. They are: Booth, B. One step forward . . . and Webb, C. . . . Or two steps back? *Nursing Times* **88** (7), 32–4.

2 Orem, D. 1985. *Nursing: Concepts of Practice* (3rd edn). New York: McGraw-Hill.

3 Marks-Maran, D. 1983. Can nurses diagnose? *Nursing Times* **79** (4), 68–9.

4 Roper, N., Logan, W. W. and Tierney, A. J. 1985. *The Elements of Nursing*. Edinburgh: Churchill Livingstone.

5 Miller, J., Steele, K. and Boisen, A. 1987. The impact of nursing diagnoses in a long-term setting. *Nursing Clinics of North America* **22**(4), 905–15.

6 Field, P. A. 1990. The impact of nursing theory on the clinical decision-making process. In Ismeurt, R. L., Arnold, E. N. and Benner Carson, V. (eds) 1990. *Concepts Fundamental to Nursing*. Springhouse, Pa.: Springhouse Corporation.

7 Omaha VNA Problem Classification Scheme. 1991. In Carlson, J. H., Craft, C. A., McGuire, A. D. and Popkess-Vawter, S. *Nursing Diagnosis: A Case Study Approach*. Philadelphia, Pa.: Saunders.

8 The North American Nursing Diagnosis Association (NANDA) has been working towards a standardisation of nursing diagnosis categories since 1973.

9 Although it is not easy reading, the text by Carlson *et al.* mentioned in Note 7 above is a comprehensive guide to the whole subject. A good introduction to the use of nursing diagnoses in elderly care is: Maas, M. Buckwalter, K. C. and Hardy, M. (eds) 1991. *Nursing Diagnoses and Interventions for the Elderly*. Redwood City, Calif.: Addison-Wesley Nursing.

Chapter 3

1 Schoenbaum, S. C., McNeil, B. J. and Kavet, J. 1976. The swine-influenza decision. *The New England Journal of Medicine* **295**, 759–65.

2 Fox, R. A. 1985. Immunology of ageing. In Brocklehurst, J. C. (ed.): *Textbook of Geriatric Medicine and Gerontology*. Edinburgh: Churchill Livingstone, 96–7.

3 Parkin, D. 1985. *Revise Nursing RGN*. London: Letts, 15.

4 A clearly-written, step-by-step guide to relaxation techniques can be found in King, P. 1990. *Living with stroke*. Manchester University Press, ch. 7.

5 Freeman, E. 1985. The respiratory system. In Brocklehurst, J. C. *Textbook of Geriatric Medicine*. 750–1.

Chapter 4

1 Booth, B. 1990. Aggressive treatment and the elderly. *Nursing Standard* **4**(26), 29–31.

2 Eliopolous, C. *Gerontological Nursing*. New York: Harper & Row, 143.
3 Kintzel, K. *Advanced Concepts in Clinical Nursing* (2nd ed.). Philadelphia, Pa.: Lippincott, 503.
4 Howser, D. 1976. Ice water for MI patients! Why not? *American Journal of Nursing*, **76** (3), 432–4.
5 Carotenuto, R. and Bullock, J. 1980. *Physical Assessment of the Gerontologic Client*. Philadelphia, Pa.: Davis, 95.
6 Hooker, S. 1990. *Caring for Elderly People* (2nd edn). London: Tavistock/Routledge, 113.
7 British Medical Association/Royal Pharmaceutical Society of Great Britain: (1991). *British National Formulary*.

Chapter 5

1 Martin, A. and Gambrill, E. C. *Geriatrics*. Lancaster: MTP Press, 97–8.
2 Norton, C. 1991. *Eliminating*. In Redfern, S. J. (ed.): *Nursing Elderly People* (2nd edn). Edinburgh: Churchill Livingstone, 193.
3 Ibid. 195.

Chapter 6

1 Walsh, M. and Ford, P. 1989. *Nursing: Rituals, Research and Rational Actions*. Oxford: Heinemann Nursing, 113.
2 Morgan, W. Thomas, C. and Schuster, M. 1981. Gastrointestinal system. In O'Hara-Devereaux, M. (eds), *Eldercare*. New York: Grune and Stratton, 203.
3 Brick and Amory (1950), cited in Dymock, I. W. 1985. The gastrointestinal system – the upper gastrointestinal tract. In Brocklehurst, J. C. *Textbook of Geriatric Medicine*, 512.
4 Billings, D. and Stokes, L. 1982. *Medical – Surgical Nursing*. St Louis,: Miss. Mosby, 977.
5 Hyams, D. E. and Fox, R. A. 1985. The gastrointestinal system – the liver and biliary system. In Brocklehurst, J. C. *Textbook of Geriatric Medicine*, 576.
6 Morgan *et al*, 1981. *Gastrointestinal System*, 202.
7 Mager-O'Connor, E. 1984. How to identify and remove faecal impactions. *Geriatric Nursing*, **5** (3), 158–61.

Chapter 7

1 Exton-Smith, A. N. 1985. The musculoskeletal system – bone ageing and metabolic disease. In Brocklehurst J. C. *Textbook of Geriatric Medicine*, 760.
2 Richards, M. 1982. Osteoporosis. *Geriatric Nursing*, **3** (2), 98–102.
3 Rossman, I. 1981. Human ageing changes. In Burnside, I. M. (ed.), Nursing and the Aged (2nd edn) New York: McGraw-Hill, 39.
4 Keene, J. and Anderson, C. Hip fractures in the elderly. *Journal of the American Medical Association*, **248** (5), 564–7.

173

Chapter 8

1   Atkinson, D. (director of the Chest, Heart and Stroke Association), in Swaffield, L. 1990. *Stroke – the Complete Guide to Recovery and Rehabilitation*. Wellingborough: Thorsons, 6.
2   Williams, M. 1987. Aphasia. In Gregory, R. L. (ed.); *The Oxford Companion to the Mind*. Oxford University Press.
3   WHO. 1971. *Cerebrovascular Diseases: Prevention, Treatment and Rehabilitation*. WHO Technical Report Series, no. 469.
4   Williams, H. McDonald, E., Daggett, M., Schut, B. and Buckwalter, K. 1983. Treating dysphagia. *Journal of Gerontological Nursing*, 9(12), 638–47.
5   Andrews, K. 1987. *Rehabilitation of the Older Adult*. London: Edward Arnold, 305–6.
6   Farber, S. 1982. *Neurorehabilitation: A Multisensory Approach*. Philadelphia, Pa.: Saunders, 258.
7   Williams, M. 1987. Aphasia.
8   Rosenzweig, M. R. and Leiman, A. L. 1982. *Physiological Psychology*. Lexington, Mass. DC Heath, 652.
9   Weitzel, E. A. 1991. Unilateral neglect. In Maas, M. Buckwalter, K. C. and Hardy, M. (eds); *Nursing Diagnoses and Interventions for the Elderly*. Redwood City, Cal.: Addison-Wesley Nursing, 393.
10 Sagar, H. 1991. *Parkinson's Disease*. London: Optima, 36.
11 Ibid., 71.
12 Ibid., 56.
13 Wolanin, M. and Phillips. L. 1981. *Confusion: Prevention and Care*. St Louis, Miss.: Mosby.
14 Riordan, J. and Whitmore, B. 1990. *Living with Dementia*. Manchester University Press, 136.
15 Ibid., 135.
16 Neshkes, R. E. and Jarvik, L. F. 1985. The central nervous system – dementia and delirium in old age. In Brocklehurst, J. C. *Textbook of Geriatric Medicine*, 312–3.

Chapter 9

1   Podlone, M. and Millican, C. 1981. Neurology. In O'Hara-Devereaux *et al. Eldercare*, 118.

Chapter 10

1   Sundwall, D. Rolando, J. and Thorn, G. 1981. Endocrine and metabolic systems. In O'Hara-Devereaux *et al. Eldercare*. 142.
2   Ibid., 139–40.
3   Schteingart, D. 1978. Endocrinology and metabolism: principles of pathophysiology. In Price, S. and Wilson, L. (eds), *Pathophysiology: Clinical Concepts of Disease Processes*. New York: McGraw-Hill, 699.
4   Doenges, M. Jeffries, W. and Moorhouse, F. 1984. *Nursing Care Plans: Nursing Diagnoses in Planning Patient Care*. Philadelphia, Pa,: Davis, 469.

Chapter 11

1 Norton, D. Exton-Smith, A. N. and McLaren, R. 1975. *An Investigation of Geriatric Nursing Problems in Hospital* (1962; reprinted and reissued by Churchill Livingstone).
2 Waterlow, J. 1985. Risk assessment card. *Nursing Times*, **81**(48), 49–55.
3 Byrne, N. and Feld, M. 1984. Preventing and treating decubitus ulcers. *Nursing 84* **14** (4), 55–6.
4 T*he Code of Professional Conduct for Nurses, Midwives and Health Visitors*. 1983. London: United Kingdom Central Control for Nurses, Midwives and Health Visitors.
5 Bates, B. 1983. *A Guide to Physical Examination* (3rd edn). New York: McGraw-Hill), 318–9.
6 Ibid.

Chapter 12

1 Donne, John, *Meditation*, XVII. The whole of it reads: 'No man is an Island, entire of itself; every man is a piece of the Continent, a part of the main; if a clod be washed away by the sea, Europe is the less, as well as if a promontory were, as well as if a manor of thy friends or of thine own were; any man's death diminishes me, because I am involved in Mankind; and therefore never send to know for whom the bell tolls; it tolls for thee.' Some sociologists have used thousands of words to say the same thing, only not as clearly.
2 Riordan, J. and Whitmore, B. 1990. *Living with Dementia*. Manchester University Press, 2.
3 Haywood, S. Standards of institutional care for the elderly. In Denham, M. J.(ed.), *Care of the Long-stay Elderly Patient* (2nd edn). London: Chapman and Hall, 12–13.
4 If the reader does not believe in self-fulfilling prophecies, or is unfamiliar with the term, it is strongly recommended that they read Rosenthal and Jacobson, 1968 'Self-Fulfilling Prophecies in the Classroom: Teachers' Expectations as Unintended Determinants of Pupils' Intellectual Competence', in Deutsch *et al.* (eds). *Social Class, Race, and Psychological Development* (New York: Holt, Rinehart and Winston, 219–54). Very briefly, they told teachers that certain pupils (secretly selected at random) would shine in the forthcoming academic year; and every one of their 'predictions' came true. This has a lot of implications for nurses working with the elderly, because we often make assumptions about how well people are going to respond to treatment, within minutes of meeting them; in the author's experience, this is particularly true of 'confused' people, whom we may unconsciously 'write off' as candidates for progress.
5 Welford, A. T. 1987. Ageing – memory and learning. In Gregory, R. L. (ed.); *The Oxford Companion to the Mind*. Oxford University Press. 14.
6 Twining, C. *The Memory Handbook*. Bicester: Winslow Press 9–10.
7 Sourander, L. B. and Rowe, J. W. 1985. *The ageing kidney*. In Brocklehurst, J. C. (ed.); *Textbook of Geriatric Medicine and Gerontology* (3rd edn). Edinburgh: Churchill Livingstone, 608–10.
8 'The Seven Ages of Man', from Shakespeare's *As You Like It*.

175

9   The entry for 'psychiatry' in R. L. Gregory, 1987. *Oxford Companion to the Mind*, 649, says that it emerged as a branch of medicine in Britain during the first half of the nineteenth century; some textbooks treat anything before 1880 as being too primitive to deserve the name, whilst still others do not consider that there was any such speciality until this century.

10 Pitt, B. 1982. *Psychogeriatrics – An Introduction to the Psychiatry of Old Age* (2nd edn). Edinburgh: Churchill Livingstone, 1.

11 Murphy, E. 1986. *Dementia and Mental Illness in the Old*. London: Papermac Health, 169.

12 Sagar, H. 1991. *Parkinson's Disease*. London: Optima 49.

13 Zangwill, O. L. 1987. Delirium. In Gregory, R. L. *Oxford Companion to the Mind*. Oxford University Press. 184.

14 Rabins, P. V. 1985. The reversible dementias. In Arie, T. (ed.), *Recent Advances in Psychogeriatrics*: no. 1. Edinburgh: Churchill Livingstone, 93.

15 Riordan. S. and Whitmore, B. 1990. *Living with Dementia*, 2.

16 Stokes, G. and Holden, U. 1990. Dementia: causes and clinical syndromes. In Stokes, G. and Goudie, F. (eds), *Working with dementia*. Bicester: Winslow Press, 16.

17 Dartington, T. *The Limits of Altruism: Elderly Mentally Infirm People as a Test Case for Collaboration*. London: King Edward's Hospital Fund for London, 27–72.

18 Riordan. S. and Whitmore, B. 1990. *Living with Dementia*, 14.

19 This survey, conducted by the Health Services Management Centre, showed NHS and private nursing home beds for the elderly to total 54 775 and 56 779 respectively. Cited in Haywood, S. 1991. Standards of institutional care, 13.

20 Dartington, T. 1986. *The Limits of Altruism*, particularly the introduction.

21 Summaries of these can be found in: Post, F. 1985. The emotional disorders, in Brocklehurst, J. C. Textbook of Geriatric Medicine, 330; Henderson, A. S. 1989. Epidemiology of mental illness, in Hafner, H. Moschel, G. and Sartorius, N. (eds), *Mental Health in the Elderly*: A Review of the Present State of Research. Berlin: Springer-Verlag, 29 (this book is available in Britain); and Post, F. and Shulman, K. 1985. New views on old age affective disorders, in: Arie, T. *Recent Advances*, 119–20.

22 Gianturco, D. T. and Busse, E. W. 1978. Psychiatric problems encountered during a long-term study of ageing volunteers. In Isaac, A. D. and Post, F. (eds): *Studies in General Psychiatry*. Chichester: John Wiley and Sons 1–16.

23 Gurland *et al*, cited in Post, F. The emotional disorders, 330.

24 Blazer and Williams, 1985. *The emotional disorders*. 'Dysphoric syndrome' certainly sounds better than the term used previously for sub-acute depression in the elderly, which was 'senile demoralisation'.

25 Evans, J. G. Physical factors in mental health in the elderly: gerontological and internal medical aspects. In Hafner *et al*, *Mental Health*, 51.

26 Post, F. 1985. The emotional disorders. 120.

27 A very welcome backlash to negative attitudes towards ageing came from many authors in the 1970s and 1980s, with books like Alex Comfort's *A Good Age*, Muriel Skeet's *The Third Age*, and others, none of which appear on recommended reading lists with the frequency one might hope for.

28 Seligman, M. 1975. *Helplessness*. San Francisco: Freman.

29 Norman, I. J. 1991. Depression in old age. In Redfern, S. J. (ed.): *Nursing Elderly People* (2nd edn) Edinburgh: Churchill Livingstone 366–8.

30 Murphy, E. 1986. *Dementia*, 166.

31 Post, F. Paranoid, schizophrenic-like and schizophrenic states in the aged. In Birren, J. E. and Sloane, R. B. (eds), *Handbook of Mental Health and Ageing*. Englewood Cliffs, NJ: Prentice-Hall, 591–615.

32 For a thoughtful discussion of this issue, see Gilhooly, M. L. M. Ethical and legal issues in therapy with the elderly, in Hanley, I. and Gilhooly, M. L. M. (eds): *Psychological Therapies for the Elderly*. London: Croom Helm, 173–97, but particularly the section on 'consent', 178–82.

33 'Neurosis', in Gregory, R. L. 1987. The Oxford Companion, 549.

34 Pitt, B. 1982. *Psychogeriatrics*. 110.

35 ibid.

36 'Diogenes' syndrome' is marked by gross self-neglect and a tendency towards hoarding; any reader who has met someone with this condition will know what a convincing defence of their lifestyle the 'sufferer' can put up. (See Clark, A. N. G, Mankikar, G. D, and Gray, I. 1975. Diogenes syndrome: a clinical study of gross neglect in old age. *Lancet* i, 366–73.)

37 Pitt, B. 1982. *Psychogeriatrics: an introduction to the psychiatry of old age* (2nd edn). Edinburgh: Churchill Livingstone.

38 'DSM-III' is the usual way texts refer to: American Psychiatric Association. 1980. *Diagnostic and Statistical Manual of Mental Disorders* (3rd ed.). Washington DC: APA.

39 McConnell, E. S. 1988. Nursing diagnoses related to psychosocial alterations. In: Matteson, M. A, and McConnell, E. S. *Gerontological Nursing: Concepts and Practice*. Philadelphia, Pa. WB Saunders, 529–86.

Chapter 13

1 DHSS. 1979. Nutrition and health in old age. Report on Health and Social Subjects, No.16. London: HMSO.

2 Pritiken, N. and Cisney. 1986. Dietary recommendations for older Americans. In Dychtwald, K. (ed.), *Wellness and Health Promotion for the Elderly*. Rockville, MD. Aspen Systems.

3 Hooker, S. 1990. *Caring for Elderly People* (3rd edn). London: Routledge.

4 Brereton, P. J. 1991. Nutritional care of the long-stay patient. In Denham, M. J. (ed.), *Care of the long-stay elderly patient* (2nd edn). London: Chapman and Hall.

5 Trollinger, J. Dowhler, D. and Calin, A. 1981 Musculoskeletal system. In O'Hara-Devereaux *et al.* (eds), *Eldercare*. New York: Grune and Stratton.

6 For a summary of fairly recent thought on the subject, see Exton-Smith, A. N. 1985. The musculoskeletal system – bone ageing and metabolic disease. In Brocklehurst, J. C. *Textbook of Geriatric Medicine and Gerontology* (3rd edn). Edinburgh: Churchill Livingstone.

7 Yen, P. K. 1986. Ten tips for teaching. *Geriatric Nursing* [US] 7(2), 112.

8 Bailey, L. B. and Certa, J. J. 1986. Diagnoses and treatment of nutritional disorders in older patients. *Geriatrics*, **39** (8), 67–74.

9 Dickman, S. R. 1979. Nutritional needs and effects of poor nutrition in elderly persons. In Reinhart, A. M. *et al.* (eds), *Current Practice in Gerontologic Nursing*. St Louis: Mosby.

10 Moehrlin, B., Wolanin, M. O. and Burnside, I. M. 1981. Nutrition and the elderly. In Burnside, I. M. (ed.), *Nursing and the Aged*. New York: McGraw-Hill.

11 Brereton, P. J. 1991. Nutritional care. 109–25.

Chapter 14

1 Christopher, M. A. 1986. Home care for the elderly. *Nursing 86*, **16** (7), 50–5.

2 For a thoughtful discussion of the pros and cons of restricting a confused person's ability to leave the house, see Chapter 6 of Riordan, J. and Whitmore, B. 1990. *Living with Dementia*. Manchester University Press.

Chapter 15

1 'Hughes, R.' 1990. An odyssey through the Eighties. *Nursing Times* 86 (26), 28–32.

2 McGuire, A. D. 1991. The genesis and nature of nursing diagnoses. In Carlson, J. H., Craft, C. McGuire, A. and Popkess-Vawter, S. (eds); *Nursing Diagnosis: A Case Study Approach*. Philadelphia: WB Saunders, 3–20.

3 Several authors, including Bloch, D. Roy, C. Mundinger, M. and Jauron, G. have used this 'five-step' definition of the nursing process. For further discussion, see the references *passim* in McGuire 1991, the genesis and nature of nursing diagnoses.

4 Gordon, M. 1982. *Nursing Diagnosis: Process and Application*. New York: McGraw-Hill.

5 Each architect of a nursing model has something to say about setting goals; for a selection of examples, using different models, see Easterbrook, J. (ed.) 1987. *Elderly Care – Towards Holistic Nursing*. London: Hodder and Stoughton.

6 Bahr, R. T. and Gress, L. 1985. The 24-hour cycle: Rhythms of healthy sleep. *Journal of Gerontological Nursing*, **11**(4), 14–17.

7 Lyon, B. 1983. *Nursing Practice: An Exemplification of the Statutory Definition*. Birmingham, Ala.: Pathway Press.

8 Schmadl, J. 1979. Quality assurance: examination of the concept. *Nursing Outlook* **27**(7), 462–465.

9 Andrews, K. 1987. *Rehabilitation of the Older Adult*. London: Edward Arnold.

10 Evers, H. K. 1982. Multidisciplinary teams in geriatric wards: myth or reality? *Journal of Advanced Nursing*, **6**, 205–14.
11 Hewner, S. 1986. Bringing home the health care. *Journal of Gerontological Nursing*, **12**(2), 29–35.

181

185

187

190